TAPPAN REEVE.

From a painting by George Catlin.

The Litchfield Law School

Guiding the New Nation

Paul DeForest Hicks

PROSPECTA PRESS

2019

Manufactured in Canada

First Edition

Prospecta Press
An imprint of Easton Studio Press
P. O. Box 3131
Westport, CT 06880
(203) 571-0781

www.prospectapress.com

Book and jacket design by Barbara Aronica-Buck

Hardcover ISBN: 978-1-63226-100-7
eBook ISBN: 978-1-63226-101-4

For our daughters, Julia and Vanessa, and our grandchildren:

Tim, Toby, Mariska, Rowan, Teddy, and Anna-Lies

Contents

Acknowledgments

A detailed history of the Litchfield Law School would not be possible without the extensive research done by Samuel H. Fisher. Starting in the 1930s, he began to assemble data on every known student who attended the Litchfield Law School from 1774 to 1833. The results of his investigations were published in a biographical catalogue of students by the Yale Law School Library in conjunction with Yale University Press in 1946.

In addition to housing Fisher's research files, the Litchfield Historical Society has continued to expand its large collection of biographical information, manuscripts, and artifacts related to the law school. I have benefited greatly from on-site research there, as well as from *The Ledger*, which the Litchfield Historical Society's staff has developed to provide online access to this valuable database.

I am particularly grateful to Catherine Fields, executive director of the Litchfield Historical Society, and to its archivist, Linda Hocking, for welcoming my questions and guiding me throughout my research. Their enthusiasm for this project, plus the appeal of Litchfield as a historic place, made the numerous trips there a pleasure.

They suggested I meet John Langbein, emeritus professor at Yale Law School, who shared with me his keen understanding of the role of the Litchfield Law School in the development of American legal education. His chapter, "Blackstone, Litchfield and Yale," in the 2004

History of the Yale Law School, should not be missed by anyone who is interested in that subject.

Mike Widener and Jason Eiseman at the Yale Law School Library, as well as Whitney Bagnall, recently retired from the Columbia Law School Library, gave me valuable suggestions about the impressive number of surviving student notebooks, which have been digitized and made available online (see Chapter Four). Karen Beck at the Harvard Law School Library provided additional background about this evolving area of interest to legal scholars.

Of the numerous individuals who have written about various aspects of the law school, I want to acknowledge three whose writings and comments were especially valuable to me. Professor Mark Boonshoft's perceptive article, "The Litchfield Network," motivated me to pursue details about the lives and careers of various law school alumni as they settled around the country, many on the frontier. I also benefited from a shared interest with Professor Ronald Chester in the legal philosophy of Tapping Reeve.

Thanks to Donald F. Melhorn, Jr., author of *Lest We Be Marshall'D*, I realized the important role that participation in the moot court sessions played in the student experience at the law school. His book's colorful accounts of two alumni in Ohio also persuaded me to tell the stories of other pioneering alumni, who contributed significantly as early leaders in many states and territories.

One of these was my great-great-great-grandfather, Stephen Upson, who was born in Waterbury, Connecticut, and graduated from Yale. After studying at the law school in 1805 he moved to Georgia, where he had a promising career as a lawyer and legislator that was cut short by his early death. My discovery that he was a Litchfield alumnus led me to write this book.

This is the second time I have benefited from the talents of David Wilk as my publisher. I agree with someone who described him as a "flexible, innovative, marketing-minded publisher," but, equally important, it is a pleasure to work with him.

Introduction

The College of William and Mary claims to be America's first law school, because it established the country's original law professorship in 1779. However, the college was closed for a number of years during and after the Civil War, and it did not open a separate law school until the 1920s. Thus, Harvard Law School (founded in 1817) can rightly state that it is the oldest continuously operating law school in the United States.

Yet, it is the Litchfield Law School that deserves the primary rank among the nation's earliest law schools. In the view of many historians, it provided the most innovative and successful legal education program in the country for almost fifty years (1784–1833). One historian wrote:

> While Harvard certainly played a preeminent role in shaping the course of American legal education, its reputation as the first influential, large-scale, systematized law school is undeserved. In the four decades prior to Joseph Story's appointment as the Dane Professor at Harvard, over a thousand young men were initiated into the legal profession under the tutelage of Judges Tapping Reeve and James Gould in a Spartan structure in the country town of Litchfield, Connecticut.[1]

Tapping Reeve initially instructed aspiring attorneys in his law office, adopting the legal profession's customary system of apprenticeship. His brother-in-law, Aaron Burr, became the first of his students in 1774, but Burr abandoned his studies to become an officer in the Continental Army at the outset of the Revolutionary War. As the number of Reeve's students increased, he began to organize his instruction into a more structured series of lectures, drawing on his experience as a tutor at his alma mater, Princeton.

After the war, Reeve's reputation as a gifted teacher attracted so many students that he decided to erect a separate building on his property in 1784 with enough room to hold lectures. It is generally acknowledged that the changes Reeve made that year marked the beginning of the Litchfield Law School. In 1798, Reeve invited a former student, James Gould, to join him as a lecturer and partner in running the law school, which continued to be operated by Gould, following Reeve's retirement in 1820, until it closed in 1833.[2]

Although the law school's records of attendance are incomplete (especially for the early years), upward of twelve hundred students came from all over the country to study law at Litchfield. One of the important reasons that the law school was so successful in attracting students from far and wide was that Reeve and Gould took a national rather than state perspective in lecturing on the general principles of American common law.[3]

Among the intriguing aspects of the law school's success was the appeal it had for students from southern states, who constituted more than twenty-five percent of the total enrollment. Georgia and South Carolina together sent more than one hundred students. The most notable of them was John C. Calhoun, who studied at the law school in 1805 and went on to a long and controversial career of public service, as described in several chapters of the book.

Although Calhoun became the South's leading defender of slavery, other law school alumni were active in the abolition movement and represented slaves in a number of important cases. The most prominent of these was the *Amistad* slave case, in which alumnus Roger S. Baldwin successfully led the defense of African slaves at the trial and for the appeal in 1841 before the U.S. Supreme Court, whose members included another alumnus, Henry Baldwin (no relation).

Despite the remote location of the law school in northwestern Connecticut, students gained invaluable experience from observing trials and appellate proceedings held at the courts in Litchfield. These included sessions of both the superior and supreme courts on which Reeve and Gould each served. Beside the comprehensive course of lectures, the school offered other academic resources not available to law students elsewhere, including access to Reeve's superior law library.

Reeve and Gould instilled in their students a disciplined approach to legal research, which led to many becoming court reporters, legislators, and judges. Participation in moot court sessions provided valuable training not just for the trial and appellate work of lawyers but also for political careers.

Another attraction of Litchfield for law students was the nearby Litchfield Female Academy. Founded in 1792, the academy educated an estimated three thousand girls over its forty-one-year existence. Its curriculum, combining academic, practical, and ornamental courses, attracted girls from many states and provided welcome female companionship for the all-male law students (leading many to marriage).

Alumnus Robert Rankin, recalling the effect of the Litchfield Female Academy students on him in 1826, wrote:

> Here the course of true "study" did not run smooth. Rosy cheeks and the charms and virtues of the purest of New England's daughters mingled with and confused the law of the learned Judge. Female rights and husbands' liabilities, Cupid and Law, female fascinations and intellectual beauties all bewildered and befogged both logic and law.[4]

Historian Mark Boonshoft identified a more lasting effect of the socializing among the male and female students:

> The combination of well-connected and ambitious young men and women drawn from throughout the nation, and the vibrant social world in which they interacted in Litchfield, created a nationally expansive network of advice, information and patronage.[5]

The network worked particularly well among alumni who were elected or appointed to prominent positions in the national and state governments. These included:

Two vice presidents

One hundred one United States congressmen

Twenty-eight United States senators from eleven states

Six presidential cabinet members

Three justices of the United States Supreme Court

Fourteen governors of six states

Eighteen chief justices of the highest state courts[6]

In every year from 1791 to 1860, there were law school alumni serving at high levels in the executive, legislative, and judicial branches of the federal government. There was a similar broad participation by alumni in senior governmental positions of many states, especially in Connecticut, where five alumni served as governor between 1817 and 1846, in addition to numerous legislators and lower court judges.

The greatest satisfaction in writing this book has come from discovering and describing how various alumni made their mark and influenced the course of events in the young republic. They succeeded as lawyers and in public office, but also in the fields of business, finance, education, religion, and the military. Some of the most interesting were those who achieved success after migrating from Connecticut and the rest of New England to other states and territories.

In their new worlds, from the frontier to established cities, they started with the advantage of a superior legal education. Better yet, they brought with them the bound leather notebooks filled with notes of lectures by Reeve and Gould. Whether they practiced law or entered other fields, their collective achievements continued to enhance the prestige of the Litchfield Law School long after it closed.

Chapter 1
Revolutionary Litchfield

On July 9, 1776, a copy of the Declaration of Independence was delivered to General George Washington at his headquarters in New York City, where he was preparing his troops for the first major battle of the Revolutionary War. To inspire them, Washington ordered his soldiers and sailors to muster early that evening for a public reading of the Declaration.

Hundreds of servicemen and civilians, assembled on the parade grounds (near today's city hall), listened to the stirring words of Thomas Jefferson. Particularly striking were the twenty-seven grievances asserted against King George III, which culminated with the charge: "A Prince whose character is thus marked by every act which may define a Tyrant, is unfit to be the ruler of a free people."

In the fever of the moment, and with the British forces threatening, a crowd headed down Broadway to Bowling Green at the tip of Manhattan Island. Their aim was to topple a large gilded statue depicting the British monarch astride a horse. The defiant act was motivated by patriotic fervor, but also because the statue contained more than a ton of lead, a scarce and valuable commodity.

Once the statue was pulled down and smashed, most of the pieces were loaded onto a schooner and transported up the East River and through Long Island Sound to Norwalk, Connecticut. From there the load was taken by oxcart to Litchfield, a town in the northwest corner of the state.

As the hub of a network of roads connecting the town with communities in both New England and New York, Litchfield became the site of a foundry and supply depot, guarded during the war by militia troops under the command of Major General Oliver Wolcott. A future governor of Connecticut, Wolcott had been a representative to the Continental Congress and a signer of the Declaration of Independence. As recorded by a Wolcott daughter, the melted lead from the statue was made into more than forty thousand musket balls in an orchard at the rear of the Wolcott house by members of his family and other residents of Litchfield.[1]

Men from the town and county of Litchfield began joining the state militia and the newly formed Continental Army soon after the news of Lexington and Concord reached them in April 1775. Among the early volunteers was Aaron Burr, who was then living with his older sister Sarah (Sally) and her husband, Tapping Reeve. Burr, then only nineteen, had moved to Litchfield the previous year to study law with Reeve, who had built a growing legal practice since moving there in 1772.

Orphaned at a young age when their parents died within months of each other, Sally and Aaron Burr grew up in the home of their uncle and guardian, Timothy Edwards, in Elizabethtown, New Jersey. Their maternal grandfather, Jonathan Edwards, was the most eminent Protestant theologian and preacher of his era.

When Sally was nine and Aaron seven, their uncle hired Tapping Reeve as their tutor. Reeve, who was born in 1744, had graduated first in the class of 1763 from the College of New Jersey (Princeton University). He was then teaching at the Elizabeth Town Academy, a nearby secondary school that educated a number of notable revolutionary figures, including Alexander Hamilton.[2]

Because of his success in teaching at the academy, which had close ties to Princeton, Reeve was invited by the trustees to return to the college as a tutor of freshmen. In the seven years he spent as a teacher at the academy and college, he developed the pedagogical skill he would soon apply as a pioneer in legal education.[3]

Sally Burr and Tapping Reeve fell in love when she was in her teens, but they did not succeed in getting her uncle's permission to marry until she turned seventeen in 1771. By then, Reeve had decided not only to pursue a career as a lawyer but to study in Hartford with Jesse Root, one of the leading lawyers in Connecticut. As a fellow Princeton alumnus, Root was likely to have known about Reeve's academic achievements when he accepted him as a student and legal apprentice.

To become an apprentice or to "read law" in the office of an established attorney was the almost universally required route for admission to the legal profession during the colonial period and remained prevalent in all states through most of the nineteenth century. While rules for bar admission varied from state to state and even county to county, two-year apprenticeships were common for college graduates, with longer periods required for non-graduates.

The experience of many legal apprentices was one of tedious, dull, and generally poor preparation for the practice of law. While he was studying law in the office of an attorney between 1756 and 1758, the future president, John Adams, complained to his friends that "his legal studies were tiring, and the subject matter consisted of Old Roman Lawyers and Dutch Commentators."[4]

Reeve, who long remained a close friend of Root's, appears to have been as fortunate in his apprenticeship as Thomas Jefferson was in studying with George Wythe. An eminent lawyer in Williamsburg, Wythe became the first American professor of law when William and Mary created a law department in 1779. In his autobiography, Jefferson wrote: "Mr. Wythe continued to be my faithful and beloved Mentor in youth, and my most affectionate friend through life. In 1767, he led me into the practice of the law at the bar of the General Court."[5]

While Reeve was a tutor at Princeton, he had the chance to read many of the classic legal texts available at the college's library in preparation for his study with Root. Most fortunate for him was the arrival in the colonies during the 1760s of Sir William Blackstone's *Commentaries on the Laws of England*, followed by publication of the first American edition in 1772. Blackstone's work, based on a course of lectures that he delivered at Oxford University, was the first truly comprehensive synopsis of the common law and its underlying principles. According to one historian:

> Because the Commentaries were more accessible to Americans than were other published sources of law, all of our formative documents—the Declaration of Independence, the Constitution, the Federalist Papers, and the seminal decisions of the Supreme Court under John Marshall—were drafted by attorneys steeped in [Blackstone's Commentaries].[6]

Although reading Blackstone's Commentaries was a great improvement over the "Old Roman Lawyers and Dutch Commentators" that bored John Adams, Blackstone warned his reader that he was

expected to sequester himself from the world, and, by a
tedious and lonely process, to extract the theory of law from
a mass of undigested learning; or else, by an assiduous attention on the courts, to pick up theory and practice together,
sufficient to qualify him for an ordinary run of business. How
little, therefore it is to be wondered at, that we hear so frequent miscarriages; that so many gentlemen of bright imag-
ination grow weary of so unpromising a search.[7]

Shortly after he was admitted to the bar, Reeve and his wife settled in Litchfield, which had prospered and grown rapidly in the second half of the eighteenth century, due partly to its designation as the
county seat of Litchfield County. The population had reached more
than two thousand residents on the eve of the Revolutionary War,
which was twice the number living there when Oliver Wolcott arrived
in 1751. However, the war disrupted business and reduced the income
of Litchfield attorneys, even though their numbers decreased when
several lawyers left because of their Loyalist sympathies.[8]

Drawing on his successful experience as a legal apprentice and as
a Princeton tutor, Reeve decided to augment his law practice income
by teaching aspiring lawyers. His first student was his brother-in-law,
Aaron Burr, who had graduated with honors in 1772 from Princeton.
Drawn first to a possible life as a minister, like his father and grandfather, Burr went in the fall of 1773 to study theology with the Reverend
Joseph Bellamy in Bethlehem, Connecticut, a town near Litchfield.

Within a short time, Burr abandoned his plans to make the ministry his vocation. Deciding to pursue a career in the law instead, Burr
wrote to his uncle for advice. Timothy Edwards responded in February
1774: "Whether you study law with Mr. Reeve or your uncle Pierpont

[Edwards] is a matter of indifference with me. I would have you act your pleasure therein . . ."[9]

Burr accepted the invitation of Sally and Tapping Reeve to live with them in Litchfield, where he began his law studies with Reeve in May 1774. From letters to and from his friend Matthias Ogden in New Jersey, it appears that in the short time he stayed in Litchfield, he was more concerned with enjoying winter sports and flirting with various young ladies in the area than with his legal studies.[10]

An assessment of Burr's brief apprenticeship with Reeve was made by historian Marian C. McKenna:

> With mastery of the law as his ultimate goal, Aaron, at least in the beginning, seems to have been a serious student. . . . Letters to his friend Matthias Ogden in Elizabethtown during this period, however, reveal that while law was certainly to be his profession, he was in no particular hurry to master it.[11]

When news arrived in Litchfield of the battle at Lexington on April 19, 1775, Burr decided to put his law studies on hold in order to join the Continental Army, arriving at their base in Cambridge in July 1775 during the siege of Boston. It was not until after his resignation from the army in 1779 that he resumed his law studies with a lawyer in New York. In 1782, he persuaded the presiding court in Albany to waive the normal educational requirement in recognition of his military service and, having successfully passed the judges' examination, was admitted to the New York bar.

Although it is likely that Aaron Burr was Tapping Reeve's first student, he was soon joined by another legal apprentice named

William Hull. A native of Derby, Connecticut, Hull graduated from Yale in 1772, and spent much of the next two years teaching school and studying for the ministry before deciding to pursue a legal career (much like Burr).

According to Yale alumni records, Hull then "entered on the study of law with the Hon. Tapping Reeve in Litchfield and was admitted to the bar in early 1775." For Hull to gain bar admission in early 1775 indicates that he may have begun his studies with Reeve even before Burr.[12]

In July of 1775, Hull joined a Connecticut regiment as a lieutenant and served with distinction in eight key battles during the war. While stationed at New York City, Hull tried to persuade Nathan Hale, a Yale friend and fellow officer, from undertaking a risky spy mission that led to Hale's capture and death. Hull is widely credited with publicizing Hale's recorded last words: "I only regret that I have but one life to give for my country."

Hull's Revolutionary War record was distinguished, and, after retiring from the Continental Army as a lieutenant colonel in 1784, he continued his military service as a Massachusetts militia officer for a number of years, rising to the rank of major general. (His later career as a diplomat, territorial governor, and military commander was notable for many successes and one tragic failure, as described in Chapter Eighteen.)

Just as Burr and Hull were leaving Litchfield for military service in 1775, Stephen Row Bradley, a recent Yale graduate, arrived to study law with Reeve. It appears that Bradley left before completing his law studies with Reeve to join the Connecticut militia, commanding a company of soldiers known as the "Cheshire Volunteers." He was promoted to major and became an aide to Major General David Wooster, who died at the Battle of Danbury in 1777.

A biographer of Bradley notes that, "there was another officer on the staff of this unit who became a long-time friend of Bradley's: Captain Aaron Burr." They would become colleagues again when both were U.S. senators in the 1790s, and later, when Bradley served as president pro tempore of the Senate during absences of Vice President Burr.[13]

In the months after Burr left Litchfield to join Washington's army, the Reeves knew nothing about his role in the abortive assault on Quebec that resulted in the death of General Montgomery, for whom Burr served as aide de camp. In January of 1776, Reeve wrote to Burr:

> The news of the unfortunate attack upon Quebec arrived among us on the 13th of this month. I concealed it from your sister until the 18th, when she found it out; but, in less than half an hour, I received letters from Albany, acquainting me that you were in safety, and had gained great honour by your intrepid conduct . . . To know that you were in safety gave great pleasure . . . Your sister enjoys a middling state of health. She has many anxious hours upon your account; but . . . she is contented that you should remain in the army. It must be an exalted public spirit that could produce such an effect upon a sister as affectionate as yours.
>
> Adieu.
>
> T. Reeve.[14]

Although it interrupted his law practice and teaching, Reeve accepted an appointment by the Connecticut Assembly in December of 1776 to help raise enlistment throughout the state. Then, commissioned as an officer in the militia, he led the new volunteers to join the

Continental Army. By the time they reached New York, however, word of Washington's victories at the battles of Trenton and Princeton allowed Reeve to rejoin his ailing wife. When Reeve returned to Litchfield from his military service in 1777, he may have realized that his law practice was likely to suffer for the duration of the war and decided to increase the number of his law students, the first step toward his eventual founding of the law school.

In 1778, Reeve taught two recent Yale graduates who would later have distinguished public careers. One was Uriah Tracy, who left Yale in 1775 to join a company of volunteers from Roxbury heading for Cambridge. After participating in the battle, which helped force the British to evacuate from Boston, he returned to New Haven and graduated in 1778.

Tracy became one of the most influential men in the early sessions of the U.S. Senate. Another was Tracy's classmate, Oliver Wolcott, Jr., of Litchfield, who went on to serve as treasury secretary in the cabinets of both George Washington and John Adams, as well as governor of Connecticut.

Reeve's third student in 1778 was Thomas Ives, a member of the Yale class of 1777. Although he was admitted to the Litchfield County bar after finishing his studies, Ives moved to western Massachusetts and served as an officer with the Berkshire Militia at the Battle of Saratoga. After the war he remained active in the militia and rose to the rank of major general, one of many law school alumni who became senior officers in their state militias.

These exceptional students, who went from Yale to study with Reeve, attest to the close ties he developed with two influential presidents of Yale: Ezra Stiles (1778–1795) and Timothy Dwight (1795–1817). Helped by those relations and New Haven's proximity to

Litchfield, Yale became by far the best source of students for Reeve and his law school. Between 1774 and 1798, when attendance records were first kept by the law school, the collegiate backgrounds of the ninety-four known students were Yale (57), Princeton (4), Brown (1), Dartmouth, (1) None or unknown (31).

Despite the work of numerous researchers over decades in compiling the early attendance records of Reeve's students from university and other public sources, it is likely that a number of names (such as Hull) are still missing. Indeed, Reeve's enrollment of students slowed from 1778 to the end of the war because of several factors. Yale, the major source of students, went through a series of upheavals, including the installation of a new president, a typhoid fever epidemic in New Haven, and, in 1779, an invasion of the city by British troops.[15]

For many potential students, military service took precedence over preparation for careers that were still uncertain as long as the war continued. In October 1781, the fighting virtually ended when General Cornwallis surrendered at Yorktown. By then, Reeve realized that he had to develop a more effective and compelling method of teaching law in order to continue attracting the best students to Litchfield.

Chapter 2

Pioneering Law School

Tapping Reeve's groundbreaking role in the early development of American legal education has long been recognized. He took the traditional law office apprenticeship model and expanded it into an innovative law school designed for teaching multiple students. From his earlier teaching experience at Princeton he believed that the school would create a stimulating environment for learning the law by attracting groups of ambitious students from different parts of the country.

From 1784 until his retirement in 1820, Reeve and James Gould (who joined him on the faculty in 1798) continually refined the law school curriculum, which Yale president Timothy Dwight praised in 1823:

> Law is here taught as a science, and not merely nor principally as a mechanical business; not as a collection of loose, independent fragments, but as a regular, well-compacted system. At the same time the students are taught the practice by being actually employed in it. A [moot] court is constituted; actions are brought and conducted through a regular process; questions are raised; and the students become advocates in

form. Students resort to this school from every part of the American Union.[1]

A catalogue of the law school, published in 1828, stated that it was established in 1782. However, a subsequent catalogue set the formal opening of the school in 1784 when Reeve moved the classroom and library from his home to a separate building that was constructed on his property.

Only twenty by twenty-two feet, the white frame structure contained a single room for lectures and moot courts. Development of the law school program was a gradual process, and by 1782 Reeve had begun to organize his curriculum into a series of lectures.

With the Revolutionary War ending and prospects for a new generation of lawyers improving, Reeve recognized the need for a course of study that was both intellectually rewarding and professionally practical. It would also have to be relatively compact and economical for students when compared to the typical apprenticeship in a lawyer's office.

In 1822, an article in the *United States Law Journal* stated that the Litchfield Law School course "enables the Law Student to acquire more in one year than is gained in three years if not in five in the ordinary method of securing an acquaintance with legal principles."[2]

Unlike the law professorship created in 1779 at William and Mary as part of its general curriculum, Reeve's law school had no affiliation with a college or university, and it granted no degrees. Although the academic independence and concentration on lectures were clearly successful strategies for most of the school's existence, they proved to be a competitive disadvantage in the long run, as discussed in Chapter Twenty-One.

The full course of instruction was modeled by Reeve on a series of lectures given by William Blackstone at Oxford University. It was designed to be completed normally in fourteen months, but students came and went at different times of the year, depending on their prior training and schedules. Some students stayed as long as eighteen months, but no student could enroll for a shorter period than three months. In the spring and autumn there were vacation periods of four weeks each. By the 1820s, students paid one hundred dollars for the first year and sixty dollars for the second.[3]

In order to attract students from all regions of the country, Reeve and Gould developed a national curriculum and updated their lectures as legal principles evolved in the new republic. Scholars have reconstructed the course of study from student descriptions of the lectures and from surviving notebooks of various students. Burton Hill compiled one of the most comprehensive lists of lectures given by Reeve and Gould.[4]

Students took detailed lecture notes, which they then carefully copied and had bound into leather volumes. These notebooks, which grew to as many as five volumes compiled by some students, became an invaluable foundation of alumni law libraries. Fortunately, a growing number of those notebooks have been found and acquired by the Litchfield Historical Society as well by the law libraries at Yale, Harvard, and many other academic law libraries, historical societies, and state repositories.[5]

As historian Andrew Siegel astutely observed:

The formalization of its curriculum, the development of a library . . . and the proliferation of organized pre-professional activities—emerged slowly over the last two decades of the eighteenth century. While . . . Reeve was clearly undertaking an unprecedented endeavor, the nature and structure of the institution was not firmly established until the early years of the nineteenth century; the Litchfield Law School remained a work in progress.[6]

To help in expanding the student body, Reeve could count on influential endorsements from former students, such as Uriah Tracy and Oliver Wolcott, Jr., who had both settled in Litchfield after the war. The rapid success that each enjoyed in their legal and political careers helped to spread the reputation of Reeve as a leading lawyer and teacher.

The law school became more widely known as alumni returned to their home towns or moved elsewhere. Many students from Connecticut migrated to other states, beginning with William Hull and Thomas Ives (to Massachusetts) as well as Stephen Rowe Bradley and Bates Turner (to Vermont).

Among the ninety-four students known to have attended the law school between 1774 and 1794, there were twenty-one Connecticut residents who moved to other states. Wherever they ended up, each alumnus became a potential "ambassador" for the law school. It was not just alumni who were migrating from Connecticut. During Litchfield County's centennial celebration in 1851, Judge Samuel Church referred in his address to a local "emigration propensity":

> As soon as the war was over and the Indians subdued into peace, our people rushed again to Vermont and to the Whitestown and Genesee countries, as they were called; so that, in a few years, let a Litchfield County man go where he would,

between the top of the Green Mountains and Lake Champlain, or between Utica and the Lakes, and every day he would greet an acquaintance or citizen from his own County.[7]

The experiences of many alumni from Connecticut and elsewhere in New England who migrated to areas like the Genesee area of New York, the Wyoming Valley of Pennsylvania, the Western Reserve (later, Ohio) and beyond are described in later chapters. Like the farmers who went in search of better land, the pioneering lawyers sought more promising and less crowded venues to advance their careers.

The best ambassador for the law school was Reeve himself, who was increasingly recognized as one of the best legal minds in Connecticut. In 1781, he was retained by Theodore Sedgwick, a prominent Massachusetts lawyer, as co-counsel for Elizabeth Freeman, an enslaved black woman known as "Mumbet."

Guided by Sedgwick and Reeve, Mumbet brought suit to win freedom from her owner, John Ashley, a prominent lawyer and land owner in Sheffield, Massachusetts. Sedgwick and Reeve appear to have based their winning strategy on the wording of the newly adopted Massachusetts constitution, which stated in the preamble that, "all men are born free and equal." Their argument convinced the court to conclude that in adopting that statement of rights, Massachusetts had effectively nullified earlier legislation, which had allowed slavery to exist in the state.[8]

The decision in the Mumbet case greatly advanced the abolitionist movement, and by 1804, every northern state had enacted legislation calling for the elimination of slavery. As described in later chapters, numerous Litchfield Law School alumni played key roles as attorneys in other major slavery-related cases.

For a number of years after opening the law school, Reeve continued practicing law while still maintaining his lecture schedule and administrative duties. In 1788, he was appointed State's Attorney (chief prosecutor) for Litchfield County. Alumnus David S. Boardman wrote: "I saw much of Judge Reeve's practice at the bar for nearly five years, during which time he was involved in nearly every case of importance tied to the Superior Court at Litchfield."[9]

After finishing his law school studies in 1795, Boardman lived and practiced law in New Milford, a town near Litchfield, where the superior court held three sessions a year at its courthouse. In a collection of his sketches of leading lawyers, Boardman painted this admiring portrait of Reeve:

> As a reasoner, he had no superior within the compass of my observation of forensic performances. I mean true, honest and forceful reasoning. In sophistry, he was too honest to indulge, and too discerning to suffer it to escape detection in the argument of an adversary. As a speaker, he was usually exceedingly ardent, and the ardor he displayed seemed to be prompted by the justice of the cause he was advocating.[10]

In addition to lectures, students could witness the practical application of the principles of practice and pleading by watching Reeve and other leading lawyers argue cases in the nearby courthouse. This experience was certainly encouraged, and probably required for students when important cases and points of law were being contested.

The prestige of Reeve and the stature of the law school were further enhanced when he was appointed as one of the judges of the superior court in 1798. He was able to accept the appointment because

his wife, whom he had nursed through a long illness, had died the previous year. However, the judicial workload and necessary absences from
Litchfield to attend court sessions required that Reeve hire someone
to assist him with the lectures and administration of the law school.[11]

Reeve made an inspired choice in 1798 in selecting as his associate
James Gould, who had graduated first in his class at Yale in 1791. Like
Reeve, he taught school before returning to his alma mater as a tutor.
Although he came from a family of physicians, Gould decided to pur-
sue a legal career, studying first with a leading lawyer in New Haven
before beginning his studies with Reeve in 1795.

It appears that Gould spent several years at the law school, first
studying and then, perhaps, being groomed by Reeve as a future associate. In 1798, Gould was admitted to the Litchfield bar and married
one of the daughters of Uriah Tracy, an early student of Reeve's. It was
a banner year for Gould, as he began his career as both a lawyer and
educator as well as marrying into one of the most socially prominent
families in Litchfield.[12]

Charles G. Loring, who studied at the law school in 1813, had a
very positive memory of Gould:

> The recollection is as fresh as the events of yesterday of
> our passing along the broad shaded streets of one of the most
> beautiful of the villages of New England with our inkstands
> in our hands and our portfolios under our arms to the lecture
> room of Judge Gould—the last of the Romans of Common
> Law lawyers—the impersonation of its genius and spirit. It
> was indeed in his eyes the perfection of human reason by
> which he measured not only every principle and rule of action,
> but almost every sentiment. . . . His highest visions of poetry

seemed to be in the refinements of special pleading and to him a non sequitur in logic was an offence deserving at the least, fine and imprisonment—and a repetition of it, transportation for life.[13]

In his Litchfield County centennial address, Judge Church stated, with pride: "After the war . . . no county in this State but few in other States, could boast of a bar so distinguished for legal talent and high professional and moral excellence, than this." Among the leading lawyers he mentioned specifically were Tapping Reeve and several of his early students: Nathaniel Smith, who became a Connecticut Supreme Court justice, as well as Truman Smith and Uriah Tracy, both of whom later served as U.S. senators.

Nathaniel Smith and Uriah Tracy had very different educational backgrounds before they became law students, yet both achieved great success and distinction in their careers. Tracy had graduated from Yale, but Smith had only limited schooling. He was turned down by Reeve when he first applied, but his persistence and mastery of some assigned texts convinced Reeve to admit him.

Of the more than twelve hundred law school students, nearly six hundred fifty attended college. By far the greatest number were graduates of Yale, followed by Princeton, Harvard, Union, Columbia, Dartmouth, Brown, Williams, University of Georgia, University of North Carolina, and fourteen other institutions.

There is no mention in the 1828 catalogue or other law school publication of any admission requirements. Reeve and Gould could rely on a college graduate's degree and faculty endorsement as sufficient evidence that he could successfully complete the course, but it is not clear what criteria they used to admit the many applicants who had no college preparation.

It is also unclear why Reeve and Gould decided to admit applicants who were much younger or older than the norm. One example
is Archibald Bellinger Clark, who entered the law school at age sixteen
from Savannah, Georgia, and studied there between 1799 and 1803.
Another was Stephen Twining, a graduate of Yale, who was born in
1767 and studied at the law school in 1796 when he was almost thirty.
On at least one occasion, a student was sent home, and, as Reeve wrote
the student's father:

> We have returned from our journey, and I have just sent
> Abraham home. I do not think it would be justice to you or
> him to keep him with me any longer as he has no inclination
> to study, he has been to school a great deal and has learned
> very little. I have this winter endeavored to teach him myself
> . . . and am thoroughly satisfied that it is better for him to go
> to some other business than learning.[14]

For many applicants, especially those from Connecticut, Reeve
and Gould could obtain letters of support and information from school
masters, clergy and others known personally or by reputation to them.
The best referrals, of course, came from law school alumni, such as one
written by John C. Calhoun to Tapping Reeve in 1810. It was sent on
behalf of William Martin, a fellow South Carolinian who studied at the
law school that year and went on to serve in the U. S Congress from
1827 to 1831(while Calhoun was vice president). It read:

Dr. Sir,

Give me leave to introduce to your acquaintance and attention, Mr. William Martin, who proposed to spend some time under your direction in your much valued Law School. From my knowledge of Mr. Martin's character, I doubt not you will find him a diligent and an apt student, always ready to embrace those many opportunities of improvement, which the institution at the head of which you preside so often present. It will not be necessary for me to solicit your politeness towards him, since I am well assured his claim to your attention will rest on a much more respectable foundation, his own good behavior and respectable character.

John C. Calhoun[15]

As the reputation of the law school spread, referrals came through a widening network of influential people. When John Lucas, a judge in the Missouri Territory, wanted to send his son to the law school, he wrote to John Cotton Smith, who was then governor of Connecticut. Smith forwarded Lucas's letter to Reeve, and William Lucas was admitted in 1817.[16]

Despite the remoteness of its location, the Litchfield Law School succeeded in attracting ambitious and motivated students for nearly fifty years. As described in the following chapters, there were many reasons for its success, which made it the gold standard of legal education for most of its fifty years.

Chapter 3

A National Perspective

Tapping Reeve's primary goals for the law school were to promote a national perspective on American law, attract a geographically diverse student body, train skilled lawyers and elevate the status of the legal profession. As historian John Langbein observed:

> In the first decades of American independence there occurred a titanic struggle about the character of American law, especially at the state level. Arrayed on one side were people who were hostile to lawyers and legal doctrine. They viewed the legal system as serving an essentially arbitral function: Ordinary people, applying common sense notions of right and wrong, could resolve the disputes of life in localized and informal ways.
>
> Opposing this vision of folk law were those who understood that the intrinsic complexity of human affairs begets unavoidable complexity in legal rules and procedures. With legal complexity comes legal professionalism. Specialists accumulate knowledge and skill in applying the law, and they assist clients both in the conduct of litigation and in the

shaping of transactions to avoid litigation. The legal profession-
als insisted that law had to be, in this special sense, learned.[1]

By the time Gould joined Reeve in 1798, sixteen states had been
admitted to the union. The original thirteen states were joined by Vermont (1791), Kentucky (1792), and Tennessee (1796). When the law
school closed in 1833, there were twenty-four states, with the last two,
Maine and Missouri, admitted as part of the Missouri Compromise
of 1820.

The first law student who hailed from outside Connecticut was
John Allen (a future U.S. representative), who enrolled in 1784 from
Great Barrington, Massachusetts, where the *Mumbet* case was tried.
By then, Reeve's role in that case was well known in Massachusetts and
beyond. By 1800, the law school had sixteen alumni from six states
besides Connecticut: five from Georgia, three each from Massachusetts
and New York, two from both New Jersey and South Carolina, and
one from New Hampshire.

The number of non-Connecticut students increased steadily over
the next two decades because of the law school's widening reputation as
well as its greater student capacity after Gould joined Reeve. Of the
roughly eight hundred fifty students at the law school whose home states
are known, three hundred six were from Connecticut, ninety-seven from
New York, eighty-seven from Massachusetts, sixty-one from Georgia,
forty-five from South Carolina, thirty-three from Virginia, twenty-nine
from Vermont, and the rest from other states and territories.[2]

It is striking how many students came to the law school from the
states of Georgia and South Carolina, and that more than twenty-five
percent of all students came from the South. For most of its existence,
the Litchfield Law School was the best choice for southern law students

and their families who sought a law school with a national reputation.

As strong as the South Carolina contingent was at the law school, the number who made the long journey to Litchfield and back from Georgia was quite extraordinary. While attending the law school in 1808, Joel Crawford traveled between his Georgia home and Litchfield on horseback, a trip that took roughly six weeks in each direction.

Most travelers from the Deep South had to make their way first to a port city like Savannah or Charleston where they boarded a coastal packet to New York City. From there they boarded another ship, sailing for a day up Long Island Sound to New Haven and a second day in a stagecoach on a turnpike to Litchfield.

When Calhoun set out for Litchfield from South Carolina in 1805, however, he was fortunate to make the journey as a passenger in the private coach of a cousin, who was traveling to her second home in Newport, Rhode Island. After a brief stay in Newport, Calhoun went to Hartford, where he had the good fortune of meeting Tapping Reeve on the stage to Litchfield. As Calhoun wrote his cousin, Reeve proved "so open and agreeable" that Calhoun began to look forward to "the cultivation of Blackstone's acquaintance."[3]

Traveling any long distance to and from the law school could be demanding. William Clay Cumming, a graduate of Princeton, had made numerous trips by ship and stage between his home in Savannah and college in New Jersey. Yet after traveling hundreds of miles farther north to the law school in 1806, he wrote his father:

> I arrived at Litchfield last Friday week after a fatiguing ride through the most mountainous and rocky country I have ever seen. Perhaps it was in consequence of this, that I felt very much depressed for several days in spite of the charms of this place.[4]

The diversity of geographic and cultural backgrounds among the students enhanced the educational experience for many of them. Roger S. Baldwin wrote to his father in 1812:

> The law school at present is in a pretty flourishing condition. It contains upwards of thirty students, and the number has been continually increasing since I came. It is composed of persons from about every section of the Union, who, though they may bring with them the habits and peculiarities of the places to which they belong, appear in general quite ambitious and industrious.[5]

As a member of a prominent New Haven family, Baldwin was obviously more comfortable in his Litchfield surroundings than a southerner like John Y. Mason, who wrote his father in 1818:

> Edm.d Wilkins & myself are the only two Virginians . . . at present; the character of our state has not stood very high here until very recently. Those gentlemen who have hitherto attended the lectures have been so remarkable for their dissipation and irreligion that in this land of steady habits, they identify with a Virginian, the idea of a contempt of everything holy & sacred, and habits of the most abandoned profligacy. But our landlady tells us that those opinions are undergoing a serious revolution, & condescendingly informs us that Va has not been so well represented for many years as it is at present. We believe her of course.[6]

For many years, southerners seeking the best course of legal studies had no regional options other than at the College of William and Mary. In 1779, Virginia's governor, Thomas Jefferson, made several changes at the college in Williamsburg, Virginia, including the creation of a professorship of "Law and Police." George Wythe, a noted lawyer, founding father, and Jefferson's legal mentor, was named as the first law professor. However, the faculty position was in the college, since a separate law school was not established there until much later.

An entry in the William and Mary faculty book on December 29, 1779, recorded that present "at a meeting of the President and Professors of Wm. & Mary College under a statute passed by the Visitors the fourth day of December 1779" were "James Madison, President & Professor of Natural Philosophy & Mathematics" and "George Wythe, Professor of Law & Police." Also recorded was a resolution that "a Student on paying annually one thousand pounds of tobacco shall be entitled to attend any two of the following Professors, viz.: of Law & Police, of Natural Philosophy and Mathematics, & of Moral Philosophy, the Laws of Nature and Nations & of the Fine Arts."[7]

Wythe's curriculum included lectures and moot courts as well as mock legislative sessions in the state's former capital in Williamsburg. About two hundred students attended his course, including John Marshall, the future chief justice of the U.S. Supreme Court. After Wythe resigned from the college in 1790, the law department continued until 1861, when the College closed its doors because of the Civil War.

Another option for students from the South and the West opened when a law department was established at Transylvania University in Lexington, Kentucky, around 1800, inspired by the model at William and Mary. One of its early law professors was the young Henry Clay, a future U.S. senator and leader of the Whig Party, who had studied law privately with George Wythe.

It is worth noting that there were at least ten Litchfield Law School students who graduated from William and Mary or Transylvania but chose not to attend the law school at their alma mater. About a dozen students from "frontier" states and territories (Louisiana, Mississippi, Missouri, Ohio, and Tennessee) who might have gone to Transylvania made the long trip to Litchfield instead.

Mark Boonshoft has calculated that roughly one hundred sixty of the Litchfield Law School students (nineteen percent) came from the mid-Atlantic states of Delaware, New Jersey, New York, and Pennsylvania, where there were also few regional law school options.[8]

In 1790, the University of Pennsylvania trustees appointed James Wilson as the university's first professor of law. Wilson, also a prominent founding father, had already accepted appointment by President George Washington as an associate justice of the U.S. Supreme Court. As there was a light case load in the first year of the court, which was then located in Philadelphia, Wilson must have thought he could manage both roles successfully.

It appears that Wilson intended to deliver his occasional lectures over a three-year period, but he stopped lecturing in 1792, most likely because of low class attendance. A similar fate befell James Kent, later a noted jurist and legal scholar, who was appointed professor of law at Columbia in 1794 but stopped lecturing after only one year.[9]

Most New York lawyers continued to be trained in the traditional apprentice system until well into the nineteenth century. Peter Van Schaack, who was a friend and colleague of James Kent, John Jay, and other noted jurists, is said to have trained nearly one hundred young men at his law office in Kinderhook, New York, between 1786 and

1828. Included in the curriculum developed by Van Schaack were lectures on various categories of learning that he believed law students would have occasion to use in their study and practice of law. The subjects included Latin and French as well as writing, arithmetic, geometry, surveying, and bookkeeping.

In parts of New England, both custom and bar association rules limited the number of apprentices a lawyer could train in order to avoid creating too much competition for practitioners in any area. Lawyers in Suffolk County (Boston) in 1788 and in all of New Hampshire in 1805 agreed to take no more than three students at a time.

Describing an important advantage Connecticut lawyers had over others in New England, historian Alfred Z. Reed noted that "by not limiting the number of students in any office, they permitted free competition inside of the profession. The only limitations upon the size of his class were his own organizing and business-getting ability."[10]

Among the first to capitalize on this opportunity after the Revolution was Charles Chauncey, who began practicing law at New Haven in 1768. He was appointed a judge of the superior court in 1789 but resigned four years later to concentrate on lecturing and preparing students for admission to the bar.[11]

The Yale alumni records show that at least twenty-four graduates in the classes from 1779 to 1805 studied law with Judge Chauncey. A number of them also studied with other lawyers, including two who finished their studies at the Litchfield Law School. One was Stephen Upson, who was at the law school with his Yale classmate, John C. Calhoun, in 1805.

The other was James Gould, who was a student there between 1795 and 1798, before becoming Reeve's partner. Chauncey was, in effect, more a potential source of students than a competitor. Both Reeve and Chauncey, however, were fortunate that in 1777, Ezra Stiles, the newly installed president of Yale, did not succeed in persuading the Yale Corporation to create a law department. A law professorship was established by Yale in 1801 and continued to be filled until 1810, but it then lapsed and was not renewed until 1826.

As discussed in Chapter Twenty-One, the Litchfield Law School did not begin to face significant competition for students until Harvard decided to establish a law school in 1817, after first adding a law professorship in 1815. Even then, its law school had only moderate initial success, training just over one hundred students during the next decade. By then, however, Yale's law school, founded in 1824, was posing an additional challenge in Gould's waning years.

Yet, as argued by Andrew Siegel,

> a case can be made that the Litchfield Law School was the only successful institution of legal education founded between 1780 and 1825; by any measure, it was the most successful. While nominal factors, such as the quality of Reeve's teaching and the prominence of his early students, certainly played a role in the school's success, the prosperity that the Law School enjoyed was no accident. The cultural moment that inspired the Litchfield Law School ensured that legal education at Litchfield would have several distinctive characteristics: institutional independence, a professional (or post-collegiate) character, a national student body, a vocational focus, and an animating ethos that transcended the personal or the pecuniary. These characteristics should be familiar (at least in theory) to anyone attending a modem law school.[12]

Chapter 4
Teaching Law as Science

Enrollment at the law school reached a peak of fifty-five students in 1813 with a yearly average of thirty-six students from 1810 to 1819. By then, the school had gained nationwide recognition and had few strong competitors.

Also, Reeve and Gould were able to teach more students together after Reeve retired from the superior court at the end of 1814 and before Gould joined the court two years later. They not only lectured on different subjects but had very different teaching styles.

Perhaps the most eloquent of the testimonials to the teaching of both Reeve and Gould was made by Charles Loring, a law student in 1813, who wrote:

> From [Judge Gould] we obtained clear, well-defined and accurate knowledge of the Common Law, and learned that allegiance to it was the chief duty of man and the power of enforcing it upon others his highest attainment . . . [Judge Reeve] too was full of legal learning but invested the law with all the genial enthusiasm and generous feelings . . . of a noble heart.

A letter written in 1812 by Roger Sherman Baldwin to his father described the contrasting styles of Reeve and Gould:

> I have had an opportunity of hearing both [Reeve's] lectures and those of Mr. Gould. For students who are just commencing the study of law and who wish for the peculiarities of the science, the discussion of its principles by the Judge would perhaps be most useful, but for him who desires a complete digest and a book reference, I think those of Mr. Gould's are preferable.

Baldwin's son gave his own assessment of his father's law teachers, writing of Gould:

> He brought to his new work [as a teacher] a keen intellect, a methodic habit of mind, great powers of discrimination and the faculty of expressing his thoughts both clearly and effectively. In more than one respect, he was a fitting complement to Judge Reeve. . . . It was feeling that ruled the character of Reeve, and intellect in Gould. Their students respected both, but they loved only one.[3]

A detailed description of the lecture experience was recorded in a memoir written by Edward Deering Mansfield, who was at the law school in 1823 and 1824, shortly after Reeve had retired (by then Gould had built a separate school house on his property where he held his lectures):

At nine o'clock we students walked to the lecture-room, with our note-books under our arms. We had desks, with pen and ink, to record the important principles and authorities. The practice of Judge Gould was to read the principle from his own manuscript twice distinctly, pausing between, and repeating in the same manner the leading cases. Then we had time to note down the principle and cases. The remarks and illustrations we did not note. After the lecture we had access to a law library to consult authorities. The lecture and references took about two hours. Those of us who were in earnest, of whom I was one, immediately returned home, and copied out into our lecture-books all the principles and cases.[4]

According to other commentators:

Both Reeve and Gould dictated detailed notes in treatise-like fashion. They would generally begin each topic with an overview of the scope of the topic and its general role in law, followed by an issue-by-issue treatment. . . . The lectures were given slowly, with deliberate repetition. . . . Gould sat on a huge, old-fashioned chair on a dais at the front of the room, from which he lectured each morning, beginning at nine o'clock, and where, students said, he "quaffs ice brandy in the afternoon."[5]

No records have survived of lectures or other course materials used by Reeve prior to 1790, but notes of his lectures kept by nine students from 1790 to 1798 have been preserved.[6] Charles C. Goetsch, one of a small group of researchers who have transcribed some of these notebooks, divided them into the Early Period (1790–1798) when Tapping Reeve alone lectured, the Middle Period (1798–1820) when Reeve and Gould both lectured, and the Late Period (1820–1833) when Gould alone lectured.[7]

More than two hundred seventy notebooks of ninety students provide an invaluable record of the lectures and essays that all students were required to copy during the school's existence. The notebooks are housed in thirty-six academic law libraries, historical societies, and state repositories. The Yale Law Library and the Litchfield Historical Society have the most extensive holdings, but there is also a substantial collection at the Harvard Law Library, which has been digitized.[8]

The student notebooks held by the Yale Law Library and the Litchfield Historical Society have been digitized as part of a collaborative project and are available online. The Yale Law Library's "Litchfield Law School Sources" website organizes all of these digitized notebooks by student, lists the repository where the notebook is held, and provides links to the digitized notebooks. The site also includes information on the school's curriculum over the years, and a select bibliography.

Among the digitized notebooks at Yale are seven bound volumes compiled in 1802 by Aaron Burr Reeve, son of Tapping Reeve. The lecture notes are written in remarkably legible script (some students wrote their notes in shorthand). Several of the volumes contain annotations by Tapping Reeve, and it is thought that he used these notebooks in his lectures during his last years of teaching at the law school.

Initially, Reeve followed Blackstone's model and organized the curriculum into ten main divisions, such as "municipal law," "contracts," and "real property." These were expanded to thirteen after the arrival of Gould and were continuously updated by both of them to keep pace with developments in the law. Criminal and constitutional law lectures were added later but were minor subjects.

John Langbein, writing in a history of the Yale Law School, stated: "This dismissive attitude toward criminal law as well as the disinterest in constitutional law underscore how totally the Litchfield curriculum was devoted to private law." He also observed that "Crime . . . was not a market that the upper crust of the legal profession expected to serve."[9]

Yet many of the alumni served as prosecuting and criminal defense attorneys over the years. Leman Church was one of the best criminal lawyers in Connecticut, as was Charles Clarke Chapman, who studied at the law school in 1818, three years after Church.

The strategic decision by Reeve and Gould not to publish their lectures was a key factor in the school's continued success for so many years. As historian Lawrence M. Friedman noted, "To publish was to perish, since students would have lost most of their incentive for paying tuition and going to class."[10]

Their notebooks gave the Litchfield alumni a competitive advantage, a point that Gould emphasized in a letter to a law journal in 1823:

> The future use, for which the pupil designs his own notes, is that of a manual or common-place book (including a repository of references) to aid him in his professional practice. . . . It is, indeed, for a time, an arduous plan of study, but it becomes comparatively easy, by practice. . . . I have learned from very many of my former pupils . . . that in their practice, their notes proved invaluable.[11]

For most of them, the process of compiling their notebooks was considered to be worth the effort, as Thomas Telfair wrote to his family in 1807:

> Now, from calculation, I find that in order for me to take a complete course of lectures, I shall have to be under the necessity of writing between 12 & 14 pages a day, besides reading that portion of the Law which propriety assigns me. Now, after performing this I have very little time; this little I have hitherto devoted to the Study of history & N. Philosophy, but now it must be swallowed up in Law for upon return of a student from this place, he is supposed to have Law at his finger's end.[12]

Law students, however, did occasionally allow friends to borrow and copy their lecture notes. A letter written in 1829 by Augustus Cincinnatus Hand to his father gave a vivid picture of the role notebooks played in the lives of Litchfield Law School students, including the need to copy notes of lectures they missed:

> My Dear Father:
> Let me tell you how I spend my time. I rise between 7 and 8, make a fire and scrub for breakfast, from thence to lecture, where I remain until between 10 and 11. Thence to my room and copy lectures till 5 p.m. (Save dinner time at 1 p.m.) thence to Origen Seymour's office with whom I read law until half past 9 p.m., then again to my room, write till between 12 and 1 o'clock, then draw on my night-cap and turn in. . . . As to the lectures . . . I can only say that their

daily practical use to a lawyer can only be appreciated by those who enjoy them. . . . The whole is comprised in between 2500 and 3000 pages. Of these I have written about 1200 and 1300 and should I remain here till May and enjoy my present excellent health there will be no difficulty in copying the whole, having access to Seymour's volumes . . . who has attended two courses and has them complete. This is, however, business between ourselves for these lectures are secured to the Judge [Gould], being the labor of his life in the same manner as a patent right.

Your affectionate son,

Augustus Hand[13]

Not all note copying was as benign as Hand's. Seth Staples (a founder of the Yale Law School) managed to compile a notebook (now in the Yale Law Library) that he probably copied from the notes of his Yale classmate, Thomas Day, who studied with Reeve in 1797. According to a history of the Yale Law School, Staples studied law in New Haven for two years and appears not to have attended the Litchfield Law School, even though he was admitted to the bar in Litchfield County. It is likely that he used the copied set of Tapping Reeve's lecture notes for instructing law students in his New Haven law office.[14]

In an article about law student notebooks, Harvard's Karen Beck stated: "Litchfield students—and worse, people who had never attended Litchfield—eagerly copied, bought and sold copies of Professor Gould's lecture notes." According to historian Angela Fernandez, "there is quite a bit of evidence that such illicit copying was widespread," but she acknowledged that handwritten copying was laborious and expensive."[15]

Gould summed up his teaching method in a letter written in 1822, which was quoted in an early issue of the United States Law Journal:

> Of the objects proposed in my lectures, the first is of course to possess my pupils of all the principal rules or doctrines of the law, to each of which I add a collection of reference. . . . Our common law treatises are conversant too exclusively about doctrines, to the neglect of principles. I am by no means undervaluing our books of authority: no one, I hope, holds them in higher estimation than I do. I mean, simply, that the manner in which they present the doctrines of the law, is not, in general, that which is best adapted to the instruction of youth.
>
> Reports, generally speaking, should be read only by way of reference, as a test to the lectures, or for the purpose of studying particular questions given out to them for discussion, in their forensic exercises. I always dissuade them from reading reports, in course, until they have acquired a pretty thorough knowledge of the outline of the science.[16]

Despite Gould's reservations, there were still relatively few legal treatises and reports available in 1822, although that soon changed. Blackstone's *Commentaries* was still the principal text used to teach the fundamentals of common law. Tapping Reeve's "Treatise on the Law of Descents" was not published until 1825, and the first volume of James Kent's *Commentaries on American Law* was not available until 1826.

It is likely that Gould did encourage students to read Reeve's first work, *The Law of Baron and Femme* (dealing with domestic relations issues), which was based on his law school lectures. Noted Harvard Law School Dean Roscoe Pound cited it as a "significant force in our legal development."[17]

In *The Law of Baron and Femme*, Reeve rejected some of the fundamental doctrines of the English common law, most notably Blackstone's assertion that, "the husband and wife are one person in law; that is, the very being or legal existence of the woman is suspended during marriage." Reeve's treatise states instead: "The law does not view the husband and wife as one person," adding that a married woman was "often an active agent, executing powers, conveying land, suing with her husband, and liable to be sued with him, and liable to punishment for crimes."[18]

Reeve aimed to make the American law of domestic relations less archaic, noting, for example, that married women were permitted to make wills, at least in Connecticut. One of his students from Massachusetts, Charles Loring, recalled attending his lecture on the subject:

> He was discussing the legal relations of married women. . . . When he came to the axiom that "a married woman has no will of her own;" this, he said . . . although it was an inflexible maxim, in theory, experience taught us that practically it was found that they sometimes had wills of their own. . . . We left his lecture room, sirs, . . . burning to be the defenders of the right and the avengers of the wrong; and he is no true son of the Litchfield school who has ever forgotten that lesson.[19]

It appears that Reeve had similar influence on a number of alumni from Connecticut who were members of the state's legislature in 1809. That year, Connecticut became the first state to enact a statute that specifically gave married women the right to make a will and devise their own property, resolving the confusion caused by conflicting court decisions.

Reeve and Gould together played an important role in developing an American body of common law, which was national in scope but still met the needs of each state. The thirteen original states as well as the additional states created from the territories formally "received" English law into their legal systems as that law existed prior to a specified date, either by enactment (constitution or statute) or by judicial decision alone.

In the preface to the first edition of his treatise on domestic relations, Reeve (referring to himself in the third person) wrote:

> His object has been, to exhibit the Common Law of England, and such of their Statutes as we have adopted in words or principle. He has, therefore, but seldom mentioned the law of the State in which he lives where it differs from the Common Law; unless that difference arises from causes equally operative in all parts of the Union; or where an explanation of it has, in his opinion, served the purpose of shedding light upon the Common Law. His design has been, to render the book, if of any value, equally valuable to all parts of our country.[20]

Judge Samuel Church, who, like Reeve, was chief justice of the Connecticut Supreme Court, said in an 1851 speech:

It may be said of Judge Reeve, that he first gave the Law a place among liberal studies in this country, that he found it a skeleton, and clothed it with life, color, and complexion. This school gave a new impulse to legal learning and it was felt in the Jurisprudence as well as in the Legislation of all the States . . .

In the more abstruse subjects of the law, [Gould] was more learned than Judge Reeve, and as a lecturer, more lucid and methodical. The Common Law he had searched to the bottom, and he knew it all—its principles, and the reasons from which they were drawn.[21]

In his book, *The Common Law*, Justice Oliver Wendell Holmes stated the essence of what guided Reeve and Gould as they adapted their curriculum to changing conditions over nearly fifty years: "The life of the law has not been logic; it has been experience."[22]

Chapter 5
Student Moot Courts

Requirements for completion of the Litchfield Law School course remained remarkably constant over the nearly fifty years of its existence. Students spent most of their academic time attending lectures, transcribing notes, reading law books, and taking examinations. In addition, there were weekly moot court competitions, which allowed them to apply their knowledge of legal principles learned in the lectures while demonstrating their analytical and verbal skills.

The moot courts were simulated judicial proceedings where points of law were argued by students who took the roles of opposing counsel. The format followed at the law school, which is still used at many law schools today, assumed that the case being heard by the judges was on appeal from a lower court's decision. In these moot court proceedings there were no juries or witnesses, so the judges and opposing counsel were the only participants.

After the counsel presented their oral arguments, a decision was delivered by the presiding judge or judges (initially students and later Reeve or Gould). Opinions were based on the legal principles involved, but the judges also considered the effectiveness of each counsel in the preparation and delivery of their side of the case.

Introduced by Reeve and expanded by Gould, the moot court program was especially helpful in developing students' legal research abilities and in framing persuasive arguments on both established and novel points of law. An advertisement of the school's program, published by Gould in 1828, stated:

There is also connected with the institution a Moot Court for the argument of law questions, at which Judge Gould presides. The questions that are discussed are prepared by him in the forms in which they generally arise. These courts are held once at least in each week, two students acting as counsellors, one on each side. And the arguments that are advanced, together with the opinion of the judge, are carefully recorded in a book for that purpose. For the preparation of these questions, access may at all times be had to an extensive library. Besides these courts, there are societies established for improvement in forensic exercises, which are entirely under the control of the students. [1]

A description of the moot court system used at Harvard Law School during the 1820s emphasized the potential beneficial effect of the experience on students:

[There is] a Moot Court in which questions are regularly argued (often at considerable length) before the Professor. . . . The cases to be argued are, of course, adapted to the progress of the respective students in their professional studies. But they are strongly urged to engage in them very soon after their commencement; it having been found by experience that no other exercise is so powerful an excitement to industry and emulation or so strongly interests the students in their professional pursuits.[2]

For some of the Litchfield Law School students, however, the experience could be quite daunting, as shown in a letter from Augustus Cincinnatus Hand to his father in 1829:

> My dear father,
>
> Friday, the 11th inst., it came my turn for the second time to come on to the "Moot Court." A short time after my admission my name came on opposed to R. Halsted of N.J. (in alphabetical order), who was an old student. I tried to cross the Rubicon, but like a poor stick-in-the-mud I could not ford. Frightened out of my wits, surrounded by a literary fog in the midst of my "nothing" I quoted from an author (Swift) with whom the judge had a personal quarrel. My courtiers began to 'snicker'—this with being on the wrong side of the question fixed me. This time, I resolved to retrieve. A most intricate question on the doctrine of relation and estoppel was handed M. Brown of N.J. and myself by Sq. Sanford of this place. The next day we had a very learned decision, luckily in my favor.
>
>   Your affectionate son,
>   Augustus Hand[3]

The author named Swift, mentioned by Hand, was Zephaniah Swift, who wrote the first legal treatise published in America: *A system of the Law of the State of Connecticut*, published in 1795. He also wrote the first American treatise on the law of evidence, published in 1810. Both of these books would have been available to students in the law school's library, which Charles Warren described in his *History of the Harvard Law School* as "then the largest and best in the United States."

Since access to the library's collection was critical to the work of the students and copies of the most relevant volumes were scarce, Reeve established a set of rules to govern the borrowing and use of books as part of an overall set of "Rules of the Office":

1. Any person that takes down a volume and neglects to return it in its proper place, on the same day, shall be fined.

2. Any person who writes upon the cover or pages of a book, or upon paper lying upon an open volume, shall be fined.

3. Any person who takes from the office any books except those which are privileged shall be fined.

4. If a book not privileged be found in the room of any gentle man, it shall be deemed prima facie evidence of his having taken it from the office.[4]

As expressed by William Clay Cumming in a letter to his father, the task of reading law books was not the most satisfying aspect of the student experience:

My time is still divided between the study of the Law & the perusal of books on lighter, but more interesting subjects. It is not surprising that the latter sometimes obtain more than their lawful share. I hope I shall not disappoint your expectations of my professional learning. But I must confess that heretofore I have felt nothing like legal enthusiasm. The pursuit of knowledge seems to be endless from the infinite number, & complication of cases with which we meet & the inelegant, uncouth style of most Law-writers renders doubly disagreeable what is in itself sufficiently dry.[5]

Because of Reeve's absentmindedness, books occasionally were not returned, but offending students still escaped without a fine. As he continued to lose books, Reeve decided to place an advertisement in a local newspaper, *The Weekly Monitor*, on July 19, 1785:

> Mr. Reeve earnestly requests all Persons possessed of BOOKS of any kind, belonging to him, to return them as soon as may be. He communicates his Requests through this Medium, because he has many Lent, and to whom he has forgotten.[6]

There were also valuable opportunities for law students to attend actual court sessions at the nearby courthouse in Litchfield, allowing them to learn the forms of pleadings and observe the lawyers, judges, and juries interacting. For many years, two terms of the superior court were held there annually while the county court sat there three times a year and the probate court was in session throughout the year. The one term of the Connecticut Supreme Court (known also as the Supreme Court of Errors) was in June, when the law school was on vacation, allowing Reeve and Gould to attend while they were members of the court.

When Reeve or Gould (sometimes both) acted as counsel in a local lawsuit, law school students must have followed the case closely to see how their mentors put into practice what they preached in their lectures. Between 1795 and 1799, several such cases were tried in Litchfield that involved a land dispute between two local farmers named Sanford and Washburn. The background of the cases was described in a recent book:

> The aggrieved Solomon Sanford . . . hired Litchfield's best legal minds, Tapping Reeve and his law school associate, James Gould, to help him reclaim the family farm through the courts . . . Washburn fought back . . . by hiring the prominent New Haven attorney and future Connecticut chief justice, David Daggett, in addition to John Allen [one of Reeve's first students] and Pierpont Edwards [another noted New Haven lawyer and uncle of Aaron Burr].[7]

As the cases continued over several years, numerous students were able to observe these leading lawyers in action. Although Reeve and Gould obtained a verdict for Sanford in the trial court, Washburn appealed to the Connecticut Supreme Court, which agreed with the lower court judgment on the facts but reversed it on technicalities.

There were also opportunities to attend court sessions when either Reeve or Gould was sitting on the bench. In July of 1790, a local lawyer appeared as a defendant before Reeve, who was then a county court judge. According to a report in the *Litchfield Monitor*:

> Last Saturday night, the Hon. JEDEDIAH STRONG, Esq., a member of the Council of State, and one of the Judges of the County Court in Litchfield, was arrested upon complaint of his wife, and brought before Tapping Reeve, Esq., for trial. At the time of trial, the concourse of people made it

necessary to adjourn to the Court House, where, after full
enquiry, it appeared in evidence that the accused had often
imposed unreasonable restraints upon his wife, and withheld
from her the comforts and conveniences of life; that he had
beat her, pulled her hair, kicked her out of bed, and spit in
her face times without number. Whereupon the Judge, after
summing up the testimony in a very eloquent and masterly
manner, pronounced sentence that the delinquent should
become bound with sureties for his good behavior toward all
mankind, and especially toward his wife, in the penal sum of
One Thousand Pounds.[8]

The value of students attending court sessions was described in
the memoirs of U.S. Supreme Court Chief Justice Roger B. Taney,
who studied with a Maryland attorney in the late 1790s:

> Mr. Chase . . . advised me to attend regularly the sittings
> of the General Court, to observe how the eminent men of
> the Bar examined the witnesses and brought out their cases,
> and raised and argued the questions of law.

Unlike the Litchfield students, however, Taney noted that he and
his fellow legal apprentices had no moot court experience, because
their preceptor

> thought that discussions of law questions by students
> were apt to give them the habit of speaking upon questions
> which they did not understand or of which they had but an
> imperfect and superficial knowledge.[9]

The contrasting success of the Litchfield Law School moot court experience is well described in an article by Donald F. Melhorn, who carefully researched the available law school records. He suggests that they were successful in part because they were modeled after under-graduate debating societies at Yale, which many of the law students had attended. They may also have been influenced by the debating societies at Princeton, one of which (the Cliosophic Society) Reeve helped to found.[10]

In December 1796, the law school students adopted a constitu-tion that was signed by "all who considered themselves members of the Moot Hall Society," indicating that participation at that time was voluntary. Moot courts were presided over by the Society's presi-dent and two other members, who sat as judges and were appointed in rotation.

The other members, in alphabetical order, took turns as counsel. The moot court clerk was responsible for reporting "such cases as shall be brought before the Society, with the decisions thereon and the grounds of those decisions, and these, if the President so direct, he shall shew to Mr. Reeve and request his opinion thereon."[11]

Melhorn notes that instead of the usual appellate court format,

on August 31, 1797, the Society voted to permit a debate on a question which especially interested them, namely, "Have a judiciary, a right to declare laws—which are unconstitutional—void?" The record of this proceeding is an early and rare example of the arguments and decision on a major constitutional issue regarding judicial review. It was not until 1803 that the U.S. Supreme Court decided the case of *Marbury v. Madison* and announced for the first time the principle that a court may declare an act of Congress void if it is inconsistent with the U.S. Constitution.[12]

Melhorn's research into surviving student notebooks led him to believe that when the Society chose judicial review as a question to debate in the moot court, the students had heard only Reeve's comments supporting Blackstone's denunciation of the doctrine of judicial review. In his view, only legislators and those who had elected them were competent to judge the conformity of legislative enactments with constitutional limitations.

In the report of the moot court hearing, a student named Stephen Twining argued for the affirmative (in favor of judicial review), that judges do not make laws, they only interpret the law. His opponents, George Tod and Thomas Scott Williams, countered that,

> The right of the judiciary to this power is argued from the necessity of checks upon the Legislature—for this the Constitution has made proper provision, by giving each branch of the Legislature a negative upon the doings of the other. As to the omnipotence of the Legislature . . . they are the representatives of the people. . . . If they abuse this power . . . nothing is more easy than for the people by a change of men to effect a change of measures.[13]

The decision of the court was two to one in favor of the advocates for the negative side. The dissenting judge stated his opinion that the judiciary had a right to declare laws void when they were determined to be unconstitutional, noting that judges were "generally superior to the . . . men in the legislature" and "better fitted for the exercise of this power than the legislative body."[14]

One of the judges in the majority concluded simply that

> the Constitution had given the Legislature the power of making Laws, to the judges a right of interpreting them, but . . . we can hardly suppose that if it had been designed to invest them with a power so great and important, it would not have been mentioned in the Constitution.[15]

As described in Chapter Ten, two of the moot court participants on that occasion, George Tod and John Starke Edwards, became leading citizens of the Western Reserve Territory (later the state of Ohio) where Tod served on the supreme court and Edwards was elected to Congress but died before taking his seat. Thomas Scott Williams was described by Reeve as "the best scholar ever sent out from Litchfield." His distinguished career as a lawyer and judge included a long tenure on the Connecticut Supreme Court (thirteen years as chief justice).

Melhorn added this postscript to his article:

> Despite its two-to-one rejection in the Moot Court, judicial review was restored to the curriculum at Litchfield when James Gould took over Reeve's introductory lecture. Two students who heard Gould in 1802 each noted that it was "universally acknowledged" that statutes conflicting with constitutional mandates are void, and that courts may, and *must*, pronounce them so.
>
> By 1803, responsibility for the moot court program had been assumed by the faculty, with Gould presiding over most

of the arguments, assigning the questions and issuing rulings on the merits . . . By 1822 . . . Gould was "reading the arguments to sustain his decision[s] and not welcoming challenges. Not surprisingly there was a revival of interest in student-run organizations."[16]

In contrast to the more passive learning methods of lectures and note taking (and copying) as well as treatise reading, the moot court experiences actively engaged the student protagonists and judges. It is likely that sometimes there were others in the audience besides the students and teachers, including local lawyers and other Litchfield residents. It is even possible that students at the Litchfield Female Academy were invited to attend, especially if a family member or friend was among the "officers of the court."

Chapter 6
Americanizing the Common Law

L awyers and judges in the early years of the republic faced a dilemma, because there were no published American reports of law cases, and reliance on English law reports was limited or not permitted in many jurisdictions. In her review of notebooks compiled by various Litchfield Law School students, historian Ellen Holmes Pearson found that:

> Tapping Reeve elaborated on which parts of the common law were valid in Connecticut. If the colony's courts . . . adopted a particular common-law practice, or if the assembly voted to make it part of the statute law, only then did it become part of the law in Connecticut. Where applicable, Connecticut officials adopted the common law of England, but they also freely rejected those parts of the law that they did not consider applicable to colonial circumstances.[1]

When Reeve was a member of the Connecticut Supreme Court in 1805, it decided that a married woman did not have a right to make a will and devise property. The court made it clear that it was up to the legislature and not the judiciary to make a change in this "ancient law." In 1809, Connecticut became the first state to pass a statute permitting married women to make wills.

The state also led the way in requiring judges to submit written opinions on questions of law to be kept on file in order that the cases might be fully reported. Ephraim Kirby, a Litchfield lawyer, undertook the task of compiling decisions of the Connecticut Superior Court and Supreme Court from 1785 to 1788. The project required a review of opinions that were filed in the six counties where sessions were held. With the publication of his volume in 1789, Kirby became the first reporter of court decisions in the United States.[2]

In the preface to his *Reports*, Kirby voiced the hope that a permanent system of common law would emerge in the country as a result of his efforts. The message was very similar to the one Tapping Reeve included in the preface to his treatise on domestic relations. Reeve and Kirby both aimed to establish a sound but dynamic basis for expanding the common law in America.

To fund the project, Kirby was able to raise half of the necessary money from more than two hundred subscribers, including lawyers from Vermont and New York. He then persuaded the Connecticut legislature to provide additional funds so that copies of the reports could be furnished to each town in the state.

The volume contains descriptions of over two hundred cases, arranged chronologically. For each case, there is a summary of the pleading and arguments of the opposing lawyers, followed by the court's decision and any dissenting opinions. There is also a section providing a synopsis of the principal legal points determined by the courts, which made the volume particularly valuable to lawyers and judges of his day and even later.[3]

The volume was published before Reeve joined the supreme

court, but the five judges then on the court (three of whom had sons who would later attend the law school) issued a statement that was included in the preface to the volume, affirming that "Mr. Kirby's Reports of Cases . . . are truly presented." Yale recognized his achievement by awarding him an honorary master of arts degree.

Kirby was widely acclaimed by lawyers and civic leaders for his valuable publication. On his behalf, a friend presented a copy of the volume to President George Washington, who thanked Kirby for the gift and expressed his wishes for "the success of an attempt to place the practice of the Bar and the decisions of the Courts on a uniform and respectable basis."[4]

The positive reception of his *Reports* significantly enhanced his reputation as a lawyer and civic leader, which led Kirby into politics as one of the principal supporters of the Jeffersonian Republicans in Connecticut. In 1801, he wrote the recently installed President Jefferson to complain about the appointment of a new postmaster in Litchfield. The position had been filled by alumnus Frederick Wolcott, whom Kirby called "a perfect Tool to the unprincipled leaders of the Federal party."[5]

In particular, Kirby blamed "Oliver Wolcott [Frederick's brother], Uriah Tracy, John Allen & Tapping Reeve" as the masterminds of this Federalist coup. The Wolcotts, Tracy, and Allen had all been Reeve's students. Despite the political differences between Kirby and Reeve, Kirby's son, Reynold Marvin Kirby, studied at the law school in 1809.

Ephraim Kirby's various professional, political, and commercial activities, including land speculation in the West, left no time or need for him to produce another volume of law reports. The task was taken up instead by Jesse Root, with whom Reeve had studied law in Hartford before coming to Litchfield. Root's two volumes included cases

decided from 1789 to 1798, which were compiled and published while
he was serving as chief justice of Connecticut's highest court.

In the introduction to the first volume of his *Reports*, Root
included an explanation of why Connecticut had never adopted the
English common law:

> Our ancestors who emigrated from England to America
> were possessed of the knowledge of the laws and jurispru-
> dence of that country; but were free from any obligations of
> subjection to them. . . . In every respect their laws were inap-
> plicable to an infant country or state, where the government
> was in the people.[6]

The law reports published by Kirby and Root were invaluable
resources for lawyers and judges and also for Litchfield Law School
students. As noted in *Law Notes*:

> In 1784 there were no printed reports of decisions of
> any court in the United States. Substantially the entire body
> of the law was to be found in the English reports. It is said
> that Judge Gould had systematically digested for his students
> every ancient and modern opinion, whether overruled,
> doubted, or in any way qualified. But vast bodies of law of
> which the modern student must learn something were
> unknown to the curriculum of the Litchfield Law School, and
> many principles latent in the common law were just begin-
> ning to be developed.[7]

After Root completed the second volume, the role of reporter was assumed by Thomas Day, who studied at the law school in 1797. The first five volumes of Day's *Reports* contain the decisions of the state's highest court from 1802 to 1813. Connecticut's legislature authorized the appointment of Day as the official state reporter in 1814, a position he held until 1853.

The Connecticut legislature called on the expertise of Day and two other legal scholars in 1821 to revise the state's criminal law. The revision was aimed at outlawing the use of poison with the intent to murder or induce abortion "of any woman then being quick with child." This clause was the first time that an American legislature had addressed the question of abortion in statute form.

One author noted that in adding this clause to the criminal statutes, the legislature did not proscribe abortion per se and preserved for Connecticut women their long-standing common law right to rid themselves of a suspected pregnancy. They also made clear that it applied only when there were signs of a living fetus.[8]

The success and acclaim of men like Kirby, Root, and Day made the role of a court reporter a sought-after position in a growing number of states. In 1807, one magazine viewed the rapid increase of publications containing reports of cases as proof of "the estimation in which these valuable records of judicial history are held by the publick," and urged more states to publish their reports in order to foster development of a distinctive "general system of legal principles" for the United States.[9]

Because the common law is based fundamentally upon the doctrine of precedent, it became increasingly important for lawyers and judges to have access to prior judicial decisions rendered in the same court or other courts. By 1820, there were nearly two hundred published volumes of reports covering courts in fifteen states, and official court reporters had been appointed by eight states as well as the Supreme Court of the United States.[10]

In states where the judges still rendered their opinions orally, court reporters, in effect, wrote the opinions. Inspired, most likely, by the success of Thomas Day, a remarkable number of law school alumni contributed to the improvement of law reporting as an important resource for the development of American jurisprudence. Thirteen of them were appointed as reporters by the highest court in eleven states and one by the United States Supreme Court.

One of the most esteemed members of this alumni group was Theron Metcalf, who was an associate justice of the Massachusetts Supreme Judicial Court from 1848 to 1865. He previously served as reporter of that court and published thirteen volumes of the court's decisions between 1840 and 1847. A review in the *American Jurist* magazine of his first volume stated:

> We will not disparage the works of any other of the numerous and able laborers in this department, (and many skillful and successful reporters there have been and are); but we can most truly and conscientiously say, that this number of Mr. Metcalf's reports exhibits all the excellences and none of the defects (that we have yet discovered) of the other American reporters.[11]

In 1817, Metcalf came to the defense of the common law, which was under attack by a growing number of lawyers who favored increased statutory codification. Countering complaints about the growing number of cases, Metcalf observed that the number of reports was likely to grow, because "there will never be an end to new questions."[12]

The debate continued between proponents of the common law and codification. In 1822 another alumnus, Henry Dwight Sedgwick, published a "Statement Showing Some of the Evils and Absurdities of the Practice of the English Common Law . . . " As Metcalf predicted, the reports of cases continued to grow while court reporters played increasingly valuable roles.

Another notable member of the group was alumnus Benjamin Chew Howard, who was a U.S. representative from Maryland before serving as the reporter for the Supreme Court of the United States from 1843 until 1862. When the *Dred Scott* decision was issued by that court in 1857, the U.S. Senate sought to publicize it as broadly as possible and printed twenty thousand copies for free distribution to the public. Howard protested that his income from the sale of his volume that included the opinion would suffer from the competition. As a result, the Senate voted to pay him $1,500 in compensation and agreed not to distribute its pamphlet until Howard's volume was made available.

The value of the Supreme Court reports had previously been demonstrated by Howard's predecessor, Henry Wheaton, who sued his immediate successor, Richard Peters, for publishing an abridged edition of Wheaton's reports. Based on a claim of copyright infringement under the Federal Copyright Act of 1790 and common law, the case ultimately was decided by the Supreme Court in 1834. Wheaton was represented by his partner and law school alumnus, Elijah Paine, in the Supreme Court's first copyright case. The decision established that copyright is not a "natural" right, but derived from statute and subject to the conditions it imposes.[13]

The majority opinion in the *Wheaton v. Peters* case included an important statement that, "it was clear that there could be no common law of the United States." The federal government was then "composed of twenty-four sovereign and independent states, each of which might have its local usages, customs and common law. . . . The common law could be made part of our federal system only by legislative adoption [and] when a common law right is asserted, [the Supreme Court] must look to the state where the controversy originated."[14]

Even though the Supreme Court ruled against Wheaton on procedural grounds, Peters agreed to a settlement in Wheaton's favor. Elijah Paine, who had engaged Daniel Webster to argue the case in the Supreme Court observed, "This suit . . . will be more interesting than any reported case on copyrights, and . . . the future interest of all authors in this country will be greatly affected by its decision."[15]

In less than fifty years, from the publication of Kirby's Reports in 1789 to the *Wheaton v. Peters* decision in 1834, the important role of court reporters had become widely recognized. They were instrumental in Americanizing the common law, while making the work of lawyers, judges, and legal educators more scientific.

Chapter 7
Student Life in Litchfield

In 1911, the Litchfield Historical Society acquired Tapping Reeve's law school building as a donation from Dwight Kilbourn, a long-time Litchfield resident and local historian. Nineteen years later, it bought the Tapping Reeve House and moved the school building down the street to its original location next to Reeve's house.

Both buildings, which were restored and opened to the public in 1933, were declared National Historic Landmarks in 1966. They are combined as a museum that the Fodor's guidebook calls "one of the state's most worthy attractions."

Visitors to the Tapping Reeve House and Litchfield Law School are taken on a virtual journey through the lives of real students who came to the Litchfield Law School. Through role-playing and interpretive exhibits, each visitor explores timeless issues of an actual law student's travel, education, and community experience in Litchfield.

Many visitors are interested in the pioneering methods used by Reeve and Gould in training students to become lawyers, but there are probably even more who are eager to learn what the students' social and other extracurricular lives were like in Litchfield. Visitors learn that law students met dozens of young ladies who came there for instruction at Miss Sarah Pierce's Academy (also called the Litchfield Female Academy).

In 1792, Sarah Pierce began teaching girls in her home, and by 1798 the school became so successful that an academy building was built with the financial help of Tapping Reeve and other local support- ers. Over more than thirty years, the female academy educated about three thousand students from 17 states and territories of the new republic, as well as Canada and the West Indies.

The greatest influence Sarah Pierce had on the development of education was through the many young women she trained as teachers. Learning dancing, music, embroidery, art, and other nonacademic sub- jects was important for those students who wanted to become teachers or start their own academies, as no school for young women would be successful without them at the time.

There were also courses in philosophy, logic, rhetoric, astronomy, chemistry, and English. Marks for academic achievement were awarded, and, as law students were often present on Friday afternoons when the marks were announced, the students were inspired to do well in their studies. Many families also expected their daughters to become intelligent wives and mothers, who would raise the next generation of competent children that the new nation needed.

Sarah's nephew, John Pierce Brace, joined the female academy in 1814 as a teacher after studying at Williams College. He succeeded her as head of the school in 1827, but Sarah continued to teach there, focus- ing on history, her favorite subject. The academy students came from almost as many states as the law students. One of the academy graduates painted a vivid picture of a Litchfield scene from her school days:

> Imagine these now quiet streets with red coaches rattling
> through them, with signs of importer, publisher, goldsmith,
> hatter, etc., hanging on the shops, with young men arriving

on horseback to attend the law school and divide their attention between their studies of the law and studies of the pretty
pupils of the "female academy." Then there were some gay
bloods from the south so much at home in the town that they
disported themselves in pink gingham frock coats![1]

The proximity of the female academy and its student body of educated young ladies provided an added attraction for studying law in
the rather remote town of Litchfield. In 1821, William Ennis wrote
Horace Mann, his law school contemporary and future educational
pioneer: "There are ladies in abundance who are monopolized by the
[law] students."[2]

Another law school student, Edward D. Mansfield, recalled:

> It was about the middle of June, 1823, that my father
> and I drove up to Grove Catlin's tavern, on the "Green," of
> Litchfield, Connecticut. . . . One of the first objects which
> struck my eyes was interesting and picturesque. This was a
> long procession of school girls, coming down North Street,
> walking under the lofty elms, and moving to the music of a
> flute and flageolet. The girls were gayly dressed and evidently
> enjoying their evening parade, in this most balmy season of
> the year. It was the school of Miss Sally Pierce.[3]

Edward Mansfield's recollections also provide a firsthand introduction to some of the leading members of the Litchfield community
in the 1820s:

The next morning my father introduced me to Governor Wolcott. . . . The Wolcott family early came there, and they and their connections were among the most distinguished people in the state. Three successive Wolcotts were governors of the state, the second being one of the signers of the Declaration of Independence, and the third the successor of Hamilton, as secretary of the treasury, in the administration of Washington. This was the one then living in Litchfield . . .

Then there were the Tallmadges . . . with Tracy and others, who had made Litchfield noted for talent and social aristocracy long before I came there . . . Uriah Tracy . . . was a very superior man, and noted for wit. He was United States Senator, from Connecticut, in the time of Washington and Adams.[4]

Visitors to the law school museum learn that before students began their studies, they had to locate and furnish a room, find a place to take meals, purchase necessary school supplies and, perhaps, hire a servant. Students at the law school and the female academy sometimes roomed at the same home, but the law students usually had the more expensive and desirable rooms.[5]

Like students in every generation, many wrote home about their need for more money, and some of the responses were probably like the one William Holt Averell received in 1817 from his father:

It appears to me that Litchfield is a very extravagant place or you must be rather extravagant . . . I have never calculated to furnish you with more than four hundred Dollars for your expenses while in Litchfield & when you have expended that sum, you must get into the stage & come home & go to work & earn something to support yourself.[6]

Edward Mansfield boarded at a private residence across the street from the home of Dr. Lyman Beecher, who was minister of the Litchfield Congregational Church from 1810 until 1826. A prominent theologian, educator and reformer, Beecher was well known for his fiery sermons against intemperance and slavery. During his years in Litchfield, Beecher became a close friend and admirer of Tapping Reeve, who had played an important role in bringing Beecher to Litchfield.

As described by Charles Beecher (editor of his father's autobiography):

Judge Reeve was distinguished for his piety and interest in all benevolent operations, as much as for his learning. In him Dr. Beecher found a truly kindred spirit; and probably no man, through the whole course of his life, ever stood so near to him in Christian intimacy. In after years, wherever he went, those families he was accustomed oftenest to visit on terms of closest intimacy he was wont to call his "Judge Reeve places."[7]

The book contains a vivid description of Reeve by Catherine, the eldest of the nine Beecher children:

He had a pair of soft dark eyes of rare beauty, a beaming expression of intelligence and benevolence, while his soft grey hair fell in silver tresses to his shoulders in a style peculiar to himself. His figure was large and portly, and his manners gentle and dignified. His voice was singular, having failed from some unknown cause, so that he always spoke in a whisper, and yet so distinctly that a hundred students at once could take notes as he delivered his law lectures.[8]

Among the many talented Beecher children, the best known were the abolitionist preacher, Henry Ward Beecher, and Harriet Beecher Stowe, author of *Uncle Tom's Cabin*. Harriet wrote of her fond memories of childhood visits to the Reeve home:

> How well I remember Judge Reeve's house, wide, roomy, and cheerful. It used to be the Eden of our childish imagination. I remember the great old-fashioned garden, with broad alleys set with all sorts of stately bunches of flowers. It used to be my reward, when I had been good, to spend a Saturday afternoon there, and walk up and down among the flowers, and pick currants off the bushes.[9]

Another writer recalled the lasting impression Reeve made on the residents of Litchfield:

> How many illustrious memories gather about the home of the founder of the first law school in America! There are other places that are holy ground than those over which a bishop has read words of consecration. Here is one of them. While this house stands it bears witness to a life that was lived on the heights. We may smile at the Judge's absent-mindedness, but should we forget to revere his memory, the very stones of the town would cry out against us.[10]

One example of Reeve's eccentricities was described in Edward Mansfield's memoir:

> He was quite absent-minded, and one day he was seen walking up North Street, with a bridle in his hand, but without his horse, which had quietly slipped out and walked off. The judge calmly fastened the bridle to a post, and walked into the house, oblivious of any horse.

Mansfield also gave an idyllic picture of how he spent some of his free time:

> In the warm days of summer, and in those beautiful and cloudless sunsets, like the day in which I had first seen it, most of the young people would be on the streets, and among them those of the students who, like myself, were lovers of beauty and of scenery.[11]

The charm of Litchfield and the beauty of its surroundings had a lasting appeal to many law students like Cyrus Alden, who came there from Massachusetts after graduating from Brown. In 1808, he wrote his father:

> I think I never was in a more agreeable, pleasant Country Village in all my travels. The advantages here to acquire a knowledge of the Law are very great. I think I shall acquire more Law information here in six months than I did all the last year. Judge Reeve, who delivers the lectures, is a very pleasant, agreeable, communicative man. It is said that there never was a student here but what loved him.[12]

A Virginian, John Y. Mason, was equally enthusiastic about his Yankee environment when he wrote:

> The situation of the place is beautiful & romantic. It stands on the top of a hill, commanding an extensive prospect, of which are some of the finest & best-cultivated farms I ever saw—which are finely contrasted by two lakes of considerable size, on which the Gentlemen have more sport in skating when the snow will permit them.[13]

As the author of a recent history of Litchfield observed, students at the law school and female academy "infused the community with youthful vitality and contributed to the town's vibrant social life—much of it centered on dances, teas, and other diversions in their honor."[14] Historian Mark Boonshoft went further in concluding that,

> Litchfield students could not divorce their collective success from the social life of the town. The combination of well-connected and ambitious young men and women drawn from throughout the nation, and the vibrant social world in which they interacted in Litchfield, created a nationally expansive network of advice, information and patronage. Litchfield alumni did not pursue their career ambitions purely as individuals but rather as part of a larger social network.[15]

Boonshoft's view is that the network was "an engine that turned shared culture into a resource-social capital-that members converted into more traditional forms of power, influence, and capital." His understanding of this significant aspect of the Litchfield Law School's history goes well beyond that of Andrew Siegel, who wrote in an earlier article:

> The Litchfield Law School was a trade school for well-educated young men, a social club where life-long connections were formed and a propaganda mill for the Federalist view of the social order. In and of itself, Litchfield was a bold undertaking. However, the Law School . . . was part of a grand Federalist counter-offensive, which deployed education, virtue, and careful management of the domestic sphere against the perceived threat of licentiousness, irreligion and democracy.[16]

In 1818, William Greene wrote Abigail Lyman, a former female academy student and his future wife:

> Our coalition parties commenced last Friday week. They will be continued once a fortnight for three months. Their sociability contributes much to my enjoyment; and the exercise of dancing promotes my health.[17]

There were also teas, plays and performances that brought the students together formally, while informal opportunities for mixing were provided by sleigh rides in winter and boating in summer. In almost all seasons when the schools were in session, the young men and women were allowed to stroll together through the town and to converse in parlors during specified hours.

According to another student's account:

> The great events of the school year were the balls, given some times by the young ladies in the school room and

sometimes by the law students in Deacon Buel's ballroom, or
in the large dancing hall of the tavern. Only young ladies of
sixteen and over were allowed to attend the latter, however,
and the law students were furnished each term with a list of
the eligible ones. Then there were charades and amateur the-
atricals, and for a real frolic a husking bee on some neighboring farm.[18]

Miss Pierce frequently entertained Litchfield Law School students
and supervised the social events. If displeased by a student's behavior,
she would ban him from calling at the house. It was said that "to be
denied admission to Miss Sally Pierce's parlor was the deepest disgrace
which could befall a young man."[19]

On October 28, 1830, Cornelius Dubois wrote to his friend,
Edgar Van Winkle, about "an exhibition of the young ladies' Seminary
in this place," adding:

> I understand from Mrs. Reeve that all the marriageable
> young ladies have been married off, and that there is at pres-
> ent nothing but young fry in town, consequently that it will
> not be as gay as usual. The young ladies, she tells me, all marry
> law students, but it will take two or three years for the young
> crop to become fit for the harvest, you need apprehend no
> danger of my throwing up my bachlorship [sic].

All this social mingling led to romances, courtships, engagements
and, in many cases, marriages. Of course, not all of the relationships went
smoothly. According to Emily Noyes Vanderpoel, while studying at the
law school, brothers Thomas and Josiah Telfair both fell deeply in love

with female academy student Elizabeth Hannah Canfield, who was known as "the Rose of Sharon [CT]." One of the brothers "offered himself and was refused" and "afterwards walked the twenty miles from Litchfield to Sharon only to gaze at the light in her window and walk back again."[20]

During his time at the law school in 1794, Ezekial Bacon met Abigail Smith, a student at the female academy. They had a long and difficult engagement before their marriage, due to political differences between Bacon and Smith's father, Dr. Reuben Smith of Litchfield. Bacon and his Jeffersonian Republican political beliefs angered Smith's father who, like most of the other prominent citizens of Litchfield, was an ardent Federalist.

A number of engagements were called off, including one between William Tracy Gould (a son of James Gould) and Louisa Wait, which ended when he moved to Augusta, Georgia, and she remained in Philadelphia.

Henry Walter Livingston was the youngest of seven children born on the "Manor" or "The Hill" in Livingston, New York. In 1820, Henry Livingston was romantically attached to a female academy student, Mary Ann Wolcott, who was a member of the "first family" of Litchfield. Her distinguished background, however, did not meet the Livingston family's marital criteria, and Henry ultimately ended the relationship. This caused a stir in the community and many students weighed in on the breakup via journal entries and letters.

Of the roughly nine hundred law students whose information is recorded in *The Litchfield Ledger*, nearly eighty of them married women who attended the female academy. One of the earliest was the marriage in 1798 of James Gould and Sally Tracy, the eldest child of Senator Uriah Tracy, who was one of Reeve's first students.

Sally's younger sister, Julia Tracy, married Theron Metcalf, who became an associate justice of the Massachusetts Supreme Court. Other law school students who married female academy students included Peleg Sprague (a future U.S. senator from Maine), Joseph Lee Smith (one of the first U.S. judges in the Florida Territory) and James Gore King (who later headed an international banking house).

These few examples indicate how far the "Litchfield network" extended geographically, professionally, and politically. In a number of cases, the wives did not attend the female academy but were sisters of fellow law students. One was Peter Buell Porter, who was a U.S. representative from New York before joining the cabinet of President John Quincy Adams as secretary of war.

Porter's wife, Letitia, was a sister of John Breckenridge, who attended the law school in 1821. Their father was a U.S. senator from Kentucky. Henry Livingston's sister, Cornelia, fared better than Henry when she married their cousin and his fellow law school alumnus, Carroll Livingston, who, not surprisingly, satisfied the family's suitability standards.

A large majority of students at both the law school and female academy came from well-off and even wealthy families. That was especially true for those who lived far away from Litchfield, because the cost of transportation added substantially to the expenses of room, board, and tuition. The parents of female academy pupils may have wanted their daughters to learn the social graces, but many chose the academy because it pioneered in emphasizing intellectual development for young women.

As described in later chapters, there are many examples to support Mark Boonshoft's view that the academic and social environment of Litchfield created an informal but influential network of law school and female academy alumni around the country and, particularly, in Washington, DC.

Chapter 8

Fading Federalists

B y the early 1800s Litchfield had become a hotbed of partisan conflict between Federalists and Jeffersonians. Most Federalists were members of the Congregational Church, which was supported by taxes on all Connecticut residents, regardless of their religious affiliation. Inevitably, politics and religion merged and caused controversy throughout the community. Personal attacks between elected officials were common.[1]

Alumnus Uriah Tracy was serving as a Federalist member of the U.S. Senate in 1799 when he condemned the election of his Litchfield neighbor, Ephraim Kirby, to the state legislature: "Kirby is, to the disgrace of this town, again chosen as a deputy, but . . . all the solid, respectable part of the town, without any preconcert or intrigue, voted against him."[2]

Two years later, Kirby wrote then vice president Aaron Burr, noting that

the [Connecticut] Federalists were determined that no official influence should interfere with their state appointments [such as] their support for the reelection of Federalist Uriah Tracy to the U.S. Senate, although he could not have

obtained an election by the people and was generally believed
to be a corrupt and unprincipled man.[3]

The atmosphere of political polarization was not limited to Litchfield residents. One law student, William Cumming, wrote to his
father in 1806: "At present, a very large portion of the people seem
under the influence of the political mania."[4]

Two years later, Cyrus Alden wrote a friend:

> There is more virulence and party animosity here than
> you can imagine. The one party doesn't associate at all with
> the other . . . the men of talents, information and property
> and of honesty and integrity are Federalists. Yet notwithstand-
> ing this, the Democrats will not trust, trade or traffic with
> them.[5]

As to the political bias of Reeve and Gould, both ardent Federalists, Andrew Siegel acknowledged that "explicit discussion of contemporary public affairs is missing from their lectures." Yet, he still insisted:

> Through their explicit teachings and the implicit mes-
> sage conveyed by the structure and scope of their lectures,
> Reeve and Gould utilized the podium their lectureships
> offered them to forward the Federalist conception of the
> proper role of law in society more generally.[6]

Many law school students had formed their political and partisan
views before they arrived at Litchfield, influenced by family members,
social groups, and regional backgrounds. Yale graduates were said by

many commentators to have been subject to a great deal of Federalist indoctrination while Timothy Dwight was Yale president (1795–1817).

In an article titled "Timothy Dwight: Federalist Pope of Connecticut," Robert J. Imholt noted that Dwight's critics believed education at Yale was "an indoctrination into anti-republican principles. . . . Once they graduated, Dwight's students went on to dispense the Federalist message." As was the case with Reeve and Gould, however, Imholt found little evidence of explicit Federalist bias in Dwight's sermons and other writing.[7]

One of Dwight's students, John C. Calhoun, definitely did not go on "to dispense the Federalist message" after graduating from Yale in 1805 and studying at the Litchfield Law School the same year. Although Calhoun remains one of the most complex and controversial figures in our history, many agree with the opinion of one of his biographers that, "having studied under Timothy Dwight, James Gould and Tapping Reeve, three high priests of the Federalist faith . . . Calhoun remained a Jeffersonian in spite of his mentors."[8]

Thirty years before Calhoun studied at the law school, Reeve taught Aaron Burr and Stephen Row Bradley, who served together in the U.S. Senate between 1791 and 1797 (Bradley from the newly admitted state of Vermont and Burr from New York). They became two of the leading figures in the emerging Jeffersonian Party during the 1790s.

The popular election of 1800 ended in a tie between Thomas Jefferson and Aaron Burr, requiring a decision by the House of Representatives. Of the sixteen state delegations in the House, eight were controlled by Jefferson supporters.

Federalists controlled six delegations, but their candidate, John Adams, had come in third in the popular vote, so some of his Federalist allies were prepared to back Burr. It is likely that Reeve was among the many opponents of Jefferson who attempted to persuade Federalist members of Congress to elect Burr as president. According to Samuel H. Fisher, an early historian of the law school, Reeve had predicted that "if Jefferson were elected, our streets would be running with blood."[9]

After thirty-five votes, Jefferson was elected on the thirty-sixth ballot, making Burr the vice president under the original provisions of the Constitution. Hamilton is credited by many historians with gaining the tie-breaking vote for Jefferson, contributing to the animosity between him and Burr that ended with their fatal duel in 1804.

Stephen Bradley returned to the Senate in the election of 1800 and led the passage of the Twelfth Amendment, which improved the process by which a president and a vice president are elected by the electoral college. He served as president pro tempore of the Senate from the end of 1801 to near the end of 1802, substituting for Vice President Aaron Burr when he was absent from the chamber.

It was the beginning of a long period of service by Litchfield Law School alumni in the federal government. At least one alumnus served as a senator or representative in each session of the U.S. Congress between 1791 and 1859. In three of those sessions, there were sixteen alumni serving together in the Senate and House of Representatives.

Despite the strengthening of the Jeffersonian party and its sweeping national victories in the 1800 elections, Connecticut's Federalist leaders managed to maintain control of the state's politics for a number of years. Connecticut's most powerful congressional representative in this early period was law school alumnus Uriah Tracy, first in the House (1793–1795) and then in the Senate (1795–1809).

In 1803, Tracy and Timothy Pickering of Massachusetts led

Senate Federalists in attacking Jefferson's purchase of Louisiana on the grounds that it was an unconstitutional extension of presidential powers. They also feared that it would lead to westward expansion of slavery and reduction of political and economic power in the northeast.

When the purchase was accomplished, New England Federalists began serious discussions of a possible secession of northeastern states from the Union. Writing in January 1804 to George Cabot, his fellow Massachusetts senator, Pickering deplored the "depravity" of Jefferson's "plan of destruction" and concluded: "The principles of our Revolution point to the remedy—a separation. That this can be accomplished, and without spilling one drop of blood, I have little doubt."[10]

Shortly afterward, Tapping Reeve wrote Uriah Tracy:

> I have seen many of our friends; and all that I have seen, and most that I have heard from, believe that we must separate, and that this is the most favorable moment. The difficulty is, how is this to be accomplished?
>
> We believe that in the present state of alarm and anxiety among Federalists, that if you gentlemen at Congress will come out with a bold address to your constituents . . . I know that it will animate the body of the people beyond any other possible method, and give a death-wound to the progress of Democracy in this part of the country.[11]

For a variety of reasons, plans for secession were shelved, but animosity toward Jefferson by Federalists, especially in New England, continued unabated. In 1805, Selleck Osborne began publishing a Litchfield newspaper, *The Witness*, which frequently included attacks on Federalists, such as questioning James Gould's marital fidelity and

John Allen's sobriety. In one issue the following year Osborne called Reeve "a wicked, malicious and evil disposed person."

When Osborne was sued for libel by a Litchfield merchant, Julius Deming, he was defended by a recent law school alumnus, Joseph Lee Smith, but was convicted by a jury who were all Federalists. When Osborne refused to pay the fine, he was sent to jail by the Federalist judge.

To show support for Osborne, Joseph Lee Smith and other Litchfield Jeffersonians organized a parade in 1806 that passed by Osborne's cell with great fanfare, followed by a celebration on the town green, accompanied by cannon blasts and toasts to Osborne. Among the estimated throng of fifteen hundred were a small number of law school students, including John C. Calhoun and his fellow South Carolinian, John Felder. As Calhoun wrote in a letter to his mother:

> This place is so much agitated by party feelings that both Mr. Felder . . . and myself find it prudent to form few connections in town. This, though somewhat disagreeable, is not unfavorable to our studies.[12]

Reeve condemned the demonstration, writing in a pamphlet: "Passion, so far as it prevails, destroys reason, and when it gains an entire ascendancy over men, it renders them bedlamites."[13]

Also in 1806, Reeve was one of six Federalists indicted by a grand jury in Hartford for criminal libel under federal law. The charge against Reeve was based on an 1801 article published in the *Monitor* under the name of "Phocion," in which he charged that Jefferson had destroyed the people's liberties, citing a long list of grievances, including "abolishing the Constitution, destroying the judiciary and depriving the people of the right to trial by jury . . . and attempting to establish a despotic government."[14]

The libel cases were brought by Connecticut's federal district attorney, and were filed with the Federal District Court Judge Pierpont Edwards, both of whom were newly appointed by the Jefferson administration. Edwards happened to be an uncle of Sally Burr, Reeve's deceased first wife. At the time, Reeve was not only a member of the Connecticut Supreme Court, but one of the leading lawyers in the state and head of the nation's most renowned law school.

Reeve and the other defendants pleaded not guilty and posted bail, but various procedural issues kept delaying their trials for more than a year. There are differing opinions as to when Jefferson first learned of these cases and tried to dispose of them. In September 1807, he wrote James Madison: "I have a letter from Connecticut. The prosecution there will be dismissed this term . . ."[15]

Some believe that Jefferson had been informed that counsel for one of the defendants, Reverend Azel Backus, was planning to call witnesses who would testify about the president's improper relations with his black slave and mistress, Sally Hemmings, as well as with other women. That testimony could have helped to substantiate his client's charge that Jefferson was a "whoremaster." At the first court session in 1808, the case against Reeve was dismissed by the judge, and the others were dropped by the district attorney soon after.

In 1809, Thomas Jefferson was succeeded in the White House by James Madison, who was an undergraduate at Princeton when Reeve was a tutor at the college. Nonetheless, partisan differences far outweighed alumni loyalties for Reeve when Madison carried out Jefferson's trade embargo (Non-Intercourse Act of 1809), which proved particularly damaging for the economy of New England.

With pressure from the "war hawks" in Congress (including the newly elected representative, John C. Calhoun), Madison signed a declaration of war against Great Britain in June 1812. New England governors then insisted their militia troops were only to be deployed as a defensive force, since their states' defense needs were not being met by the federal government.

For southern law students like Augustus B. Longstreet of Georgia, it was difficult to understand the widespread opposition of New England to the war in 1813 when there was such strong support for it in the South. Based on the calls of newspapers like the *Connecticut Currant* for withholding taxes and declaring neutrality, Longstreet became convinced that New England was on the point of seceding from the Union.[16]

As one historian summarized the conditions in New England at the end of 1814:

> It was in this atmosphere of long-standing partisanship, the failures and misery of the war and the heavily strained bonds of national unity, that the seeds of the Hartford Convention sprouted. . . . The convention was held in Hartford in December, 1814, and was attended by twenty-six representatives from Massachusetts, Connecticut, Rhode Island, New Hampshire, and Vermont. But the delegates—all professional politicians and party leaders—turned out to be considerably more moderate and less radical than the rank-and-file of New England Federalism.[17]

Reeve, who was then the chief justice of the Connecticut Supreme Court, was not a delegate to the convention. It is very likely, however, that he closely followed the secret proceedings through two of the seven delegates from Connecticut who were law school alumni. Nathaniel Smith was an associate justice of the state's supreme court and Roger Minot Sherman was then a state senator, who would later also serve on the high court.

Though some of the delegates are said to have called for the region's secession from the Union, the moderates prevailed. The final report included only veiled references to possible reasons for disunion, but the Jeffersonian press attacked the convention as treasonous. As it turned out, the convention was largely ignored by the general public in the midst of euphoria over the victory of General Andrew Jackson at the Battle of New Orleans and the conclusion of a peace treaty with Britain in January 1815. Many historians believe that the Federalist Party never recovered from the public's negative views of the Hartford Convention.

Connecticut remained one of the last bastions of Federalism for several more years, as shown in a letter written by John Y. Mason to his father in January 1818:

> The political complexion of the state is undergoing a rapid change—the Democrats . . . already have a Republican governor and the lower house & it is expected will have a senate of the same principles the next winter. . . . The state was [torn] here for a long time under the religious and political direction of the Federalists. . . . The first event, in order of time, which shook their long established power, was the Hartford Convention.[18]

The new governor mentioned by Mason was Oliver Wolcott, Jr., a Litchfield resident and one of Reeve's earliest students. Wolcott ran as a "Toleration Republican" in 1817 and defeated the candidate of the Federalist Party, to which Wolcott had long belonged. Annually reelected until 1826, Wolcott also presided over the convention that framed the state's first constitution in 1818, which disestablished the Congregational church in Connecticut and introduced other important reforms.

From research done by Mark Boonshoft it appears that there were fifty-eight law school alumni elected to the U.S. House of Representatives (some served multiple terms) up to 1823, when the Federalist Party had effectively disappeared. Of these, twenty-four were identified as Federalists, thirty-three as Republicans (Jeffersonians) and one was a supporter of John Quincy Adams.[19]

As the Federalists faded from the political scene, forty-nine additional alumni were elected to the U.S. House of Representatives in the coming years as candidates of various political parties, including Anti-Jacksonian, Anti-Masonic, Democrat, Free-Soil, Jacksonian and Whig. The roles played by many alumni in all branches of the government at the national level are described in later chapters.

Chapter 9

Slavery

Tapping Reeve's role in winning the 1781 case that freed the slave known as "Mumbet" gained him wide recognition as both a leading abolitionist and a legal scholar. The trial court's decision became a precedent for the Massachusetts Supreme Court's ruling two years later that slavery was prohibited by the terms of the state's constitution, adopted in 1780.

Most of the New England states passed laws in the 1780s providing for gradual abolition of slavery. Connecticut's Gradual Abolition Act, however, emancipated only those who were born into slavery after its enactment in 1784 and once they reached the age of twenty-five (later reduced to twenty-one).

Most students arrived at the law school with their attitudes toward slavery and abolition strongly influenced by their regional and family backgrounds. On the subject of slavery, Reeve and Gould did not hesitate to make their own positions clear to their students, as described in an excellent book by Ellen Holmes Pearson:

> Although Gould made his antislavery leanings known, he did not try to hide the fact that the institution was still legal in Connecticut. . . . Gould was aware that his mentor,

Tapping Reeve, opposed the conception of slavery in Connecticut as legal . . . and while he did not want to undermine Reeve's authority, Gould's students needed to understand the law, not what Reeve believed the law ought to be.[1]

Pearson discovered that Asa Bacon, who was a student at the law school in 1794, wrote in his notebook that Reeve deemed the institution of slavery "founded in violence and contrary to the laws of natural justice." Ely Warner wrote in his 1808 notebook that Gould said Reeve was so much "opposed to this practice on the grounds of natural law," that he was "unwilling to acknowledge that Connecticut law explicitly countenanced slavery."[2]

A document recently sold to a collector revealed that in 1790 Reeve and six others agreed in writing to seek an end to slavery in Connecticut through a "judicial determination . . . of whether any Negro can be legally holden in slavery in this state unless sentenced thereto agreeably to positive law or subjected thereto by his or her voluntary contract . . ."

The subscribers agreed "to defray the expense which may arise in any action or actions to be commenced for that purpose . . ." Shortly after signing that document, Reeve joined the Connecticut Supreme Court, and there is no indication that the signatories ever actively pursued their goal. It was not until 1848 that Connecticut finally abolished slavery.[3]

In his 1816 treatise on domestic relations, *Law of Baron and Femme*, Reeve softened his criticism of Connecticut's slavery laws when he wrote:

The law, as heretofore practiced in this State respecting slaves, must now be uninteresting. I will, however, lest the slavery that prevailed in this State should be forgotten, mention some things which show that Slavery here was very far from being of the absolute rigid kind. . . . From the whole, we see that slaves had the same right of life and property as apprentices and the difference betwixt them was this: an apprentice is a servant for a time, and the slave is a servant for life.[4]

According to the 1790 census report, there were 3,763 slaves in New England, including 2,648 in Connecticut, but none in Massachusetts or Vermont. New York's 21,324 slaves accounted for nearly half the total number in the four Middle Atlantic states. Of the roughly 650,000 slaves in the southern states, Virginia had nearly 300,000 while Maryland, North Carolina, and South Carolina had about 100,000 each.[5]

The 1790 census for Litchfield County included one hundred ninety-two "non-white free people" and eighty-eight slaves. The listing for Tapping Reeve showed neither slaves nor non-white free people living in his household. Marian McKenna stated in her book that prior to the death of Sally Reeve in 1797, the Reeves "had servants and, on occasion, slaves, evidently the property of Sally's brother [Aaron Burr], who sent them from New York to Litchfield." Burr was known to have owned slaves, but, in view of Reeve's strong abolitionist views, it is highly unlikely that Reeve would have owned or employed a slave.[6]

The census data did not include runaway slaves, such as William Grimes, a remarkable man, who arrived in Litchfield sometime after 1814. Details about his life are a blend of facts and lore, based mainly on a memoir he wrote and published in 1825. He was born a slave in

Virginia and, after being severely mistreated by several masters, he escaped in 1814 by stowing away on a ship bound for New York. From there Grimes moved eventually to New Haven, where he found work as a barber and servant, mainly to Yale students. As he wrote in his memoir:

> I then went to work about the Colleges . . . also, shaving, cutting hair, &c. such as waiting on the scholars in their rooms, and all other kinds of work that I could do when not employed at this. I worked about the Colleges about six or eight months. I had then accumulated about fifty dollars, and hearing that there was no barber in Litchfield, (a very pleasant town, about 36 miles back in the country, where the celebrated Law school, under the direction of Tapping Reeve Esq. was kept,) and as there were between twenty and thirty law students, I thought it a good place for me. I accordingly went and established myself as a barber. I very soon had a great deal of custom, amounting to fifty or sixty dollars per month.[7]

Grimes married, raised a family, and owned property in Litchfield. Eventually, some of the southern students at the law school learned of his runaway status and notified his master in Savannah, who took steps to recover him. Two Litchfield residents and some law students helped him dispose of his property and used the proceeds to purchase his freedom. Toward the end of his memoir, he wrote:

> I have to thank my master, however, that he took what I had, and freed me. . . . How my heart did rejoice, and thank God! From what anxiety, what pain and heart ache did it

relieve me . . . the thought of being snatched up and taken
back, was awful. Accustomed as I had been to freedom, for
years, the miseries of slavery which I had felt, and knew, and
tasted, were presented to my mind in no faint image.[8]

Some of the southern alumni owned a large number of slaves,
including Josiah Collins III, who came from a wealthy North Carolina
family. After graduating from Harvard College and attending the law
school in 1826, he returned to North Carolina and inherited a large
plantation. By 1860, his four thousand acres were worked by more
than three hundred slaves. The plantation was destroyed by Union
troops during the Civil War, but it was later restored as a state historic
site, demonstrating the plantation life of slaves.

A more typical slave-owning alumnus was William Nuttall, who
came to the law school in 1823 from North Carolina. In 1832, he purchased a plantation outside of Tallahassee, Florida, which grew cotton
and housed over fifty slaves. There were many others who owned relatively few slaves but made their living mainly as lawyers, such as Han-
nibal Chandler, who was the prosecuting attorney for Westmoreland
County, Virginia, for most of his life.

The southern alumnus with the most unusual background was
Moses Aaron Simons. Members of his extended Jewish family owned
considerable property near Charleston, South Carolina, as well as
numerous slaves. Simons attended Yale in the class of 1809 and was its
first Jewish graduate. That was a notable achievement in itself, but
recent research has uncovered the possibility that his mother may have
been a black slave or servant of his father. If so, it would have made him
also the first African American graduate of Yale and the only known
black alumnus of the Litchfield Law School, which he attended in 1810.

In December 1817, while he was working as a young lawyer in New York City, Simons and his brother were asked to leave a public dance by the host, who had received complaints from other attendees about the presence of the "colored" men. At a subsequent dance, an altercation with the same host led to Simons being arrested and charged with assault.

At his trial, Simons was well supported by a number of character witnesses but was found guilty of the assault and assessed a small fine. Newspaper comments about the racial implications of the case undermined Simon's professional standing among members of the bar. His career declined after the trial, and in 1821 he moved to London, where he is believed to have died in 1822.[9]

An impressive number of law school alumni used their legal and political skills to advance the rights and protections of African Americans in the South as well as North. In 1823, alumnus John Young Mason (a future U.S. attorney general) was assigned by the County Court in Greensville, Virginia, to represent "Scipio," a slave accused of breaking into a store and taking merchandise, money, and bonds. The court paid Mason twenty-five dollars to represent Scipio, and he skillfully won an acquittal in the case.

Due to the efforts of alumnus Stephen Upson, a prominent Georgia state representative, Austin Dabney became the only African American to be granted land by the state of Georgia in recognition of his military service during the Revolution. The legislature also provided seventy pounds to emancipate Dabney from his owner, who had sent Dabney to serve with the state militia as his substitute.

In upstate New York, two alumni, Abraham Bruyn Hasbrouck and Charles H. Ruggles, helped reunite a freed slave, called "Sojourner Truth," with her young son, who had been illegally sold to a slaveholder in Alabama. Hasbrouck and Ruggles, who were law partners, won a landmark case for Sojourner Truth, who went on to become a noted abolitionist and advocate of women's rights.

In 1833, alumnus William Wolcott Ellsworth (a future Connecticut governor) defended Prudence Crandall, a white school teacher who was tried for breaking the state's "Black Law," because she admitted young black women to her school in Canterbury. Her conviction in a lower court was reversed on a technicality by the state supreme court, which included two Litchfield Law School alumni, Samuel Church and Thomas Williams. The case raised the important question of whether blacks were citizens under the U.S. Constitution. The trial court judge, David Daggett, advised the jury:

> To my mind, it would be a perversion of terms to say that slaves, free blacks or Indians were citizens, as the term is used in the Constitution. God forbid that I should add to the degradation of this race of men, but I am bound by my duty to say they are not citizens.

In 1857, U.S. Supreme Court Justice Roger Taney cited Daggett's statement when he wrote the decisive opinion in the *Dred Scott* case, finding that blacks could not be citizens and also that states had the right to decide whether to allow slavery. Taney said that Daggett's ruling in the Crandall case was noteworthy because Connecticut then had a reputation as a liberal state.[10]

The cause of the abolitionists suffered a major setback in the *Anthony Burns* case, which tested the constitutionality of the Fugitive Slave Law of 1850. Burns was a fugitive slave who escaped to Boston, where he was arrested in 1854. His case was brought before alumnus Edward Greely Loring, a federal commissioner, who was then serving also as a probate judge as well as a lecturer at Harvard Law School.

Although there was intense anti-slavery feeling in Massachusetts, Loring ruled that under the law, Burns had to be returned to his owner in Virginia. This decision would haunt him for the rest of his career in Massachusetts and, in 1858, he was removed from his judicial position by the governor of Massachusetts because of pressure from the legislature.

The *Burns* decision made Loring a hero in the South, and President Buchanan named him to the Court of Claims in Washington in 1858, where he served until he retired from public life in 1877. When abolitionists in Boston purchased Burns from his owner, he returned to Massachusetts a free man. Burns attended Oberlin College in Ohio on a scholarship and later served as a minister in Canada until his early death from tuberculosis at the age of twenty-eight.

The decision in a New York slavery case by another alumnus, Judge Elijah Paine, made him a hero in the North and a villain in the South. In 1852, a Virginia family named Lemmon traveled to New York City with their eight slaves. A freed African American tried to emancipate the slaves by filing a petition with Judge Paine, who ruled that the Lemmon slaves were entitled to their freedom under New York Law. He also held that the Fugitive Slave Act did not apply because they were not fugitives. After two appeals, New York's highest court upheld his verdict in 1860 with the strongest statement against slavery of any state's highest court prior to the Civil War.

Among the numerous alumni who championed the cause of abolitionism, there was none more ardent than Horace Mann. Although he is best known as a leading educational reformer, he was also a Whig politician and was elected in 1848 to the U.S. Congress. In his first speech he argued strongly that it was the right and duty of Congress to exclude slavery from the territories.

During his first term, Mann volunteered as counsel for two men who were indicted for aiding seventy-seven slaves in the District of Columbia. The slaves had attempted to escape on a schooner named the *Pearl* but were captured and returned to their owners.

Although Mann's clients were found guilty, the case led Congress to end the slave trade in the District of Columbia, but it did not abolish slavery there. Prohibiting the slave trade was a provision of the Compromise of 1850, which dealt primarily with the issue of whether new states would be admitted to the Union as "slave" or "free" states (see Chapter Twenty).

One of the most notable of the alumni abolitionists was Roger Sherman Baldwin. He once defended and secured the freedom of a runaway slave and later stood up to an angry crowd who opposed the building of a training school for African Americans in New Haven. He is best known, however, for his role in the famous *Amistad* case, in which he successfully defended captive African slaves who had revolted on the schooner *Amistad*. The slaves were charged with murder and piracy because they had seized the ship off the coast of Cuba and killed the captain as well as the cook.

The remaining crew members were ordered to sail back to Africa, but they secretly steered the *Amistad* north until it was stopped by a U.S. naval vessel off the Connecticut coast. Baldwin won the case for the slaves in the trial court, but the U.S. government appealed the decision to the U.S. Supreme Court. As described in Chapter Sixteen, the verdict in favor of the Africans was upheld by the Supreme Court, which included another alumnus, Justice Henry Baldwin.

In addition to the important roles played by alumni in numerous slavery cases, alumni members of Congress were increasingly confronted with slavery issues, beginning with the bitter debate over Missouri's application for admission to the Union in 1819. Among the members of Congress at that time were ten alumni (six northerners and four southerners).

The northern delegations, led by Senator Rufus King of New York (father of two alumni), argued that Congress had the power to prohibit slavery in a new state. Southerners argued that new states had the freedom to choose slavery if they wished. One of their leaders in the House was alumnus Eldred Simkins from South Carolina, who had filled a seat vacated by his friend, John C. Calhoun, after he resigned to become Secretary of War in Monroe's cabinet.

Although the Senate and the House passed different bills, a compromise was worked out in 1820, admitting Missouri as a slave state together with Maine (formerly part of Massachusetts) as a free state. The compromise was widely criticized in both the South and North, but it helped to hold the Union together for more than thirty years.

Chapter 10
Westward Ho!

Long before Horace Greely issued his call to "go west young man," numerous Litchfield Law School alumni had emigrated to the newer states and territories. They carried with them Blackstone's *Commentaries* and their law school notebooks, filled with common law principles that were as applicable in Litchfield Township, Ohio, as in Litchfield, Connecticut.

Before heading west and south, most of these alumni had already been admitted to the bar either in Litchfield or in their home states. They also carried a prized certificate, attesting to their completion of the law school course. The one issued to Henry Starr, who was admitted to the bar in Troy, New York, before moving to Cincinnati, read:

> 10, August 1810, Mr. Henry Starr read law in my office and constantly attended the lectures there delivered from the 24th day of October 1809 to the 10th day of August 1810. Tapping Reeve.[1]

The destination for many of the pioneers was part of the Northwest Territory in what is now northeastern Ohio. It was then called "New Connecticut" by some and Connecticut's "Western Reserve" by others.

The Reserve had been granted to the Colony of Connecticut under the terms of its charter by King Charles II. Following the Revolutionary War, the State of Connecticut exchanged part of its western lands to the federal government in return for federal assumption of its debt.

To raise funds for public education, the state began in 1795 to sell the remaining part of the Western Reserve, which stretched from Pennsylvania's western border for one hundred twenty miles along the southern shore of Lake Erie. The purchaser was a large group of Connecticut investors, calling themselves the Connecticut Land Company, who planned to divide the land and sell it to settlers.

Among the investors were a number of men who were alumni or otherwise connected with the law school. One of the largest shareholders was Pierpont Edwards, whose son, John Starke Edwards, studied with Reeve in 1796. Representing his father, the younger Edwards moved to the Western Reserve in 1799 and was instrumental in settling a large area about sixty miles east of present-day Cleveland.

He was accompanied on that journey by a number of men, including George Tod, a contemporary at the law school who had participated with him in the moot court proceedings described in Chapter Five. Edwards and Tod were both admitted to the bar in 1800 at the Trumbull County seat of Warren and were among the first lawyers in the Western Reserve. They were followed a few years later by another alumnus, Homer Hine, who settled in Youngstown along with Tod.

Shortly after their bar admission, Edwards and Tod became involved as opposing counsel in a complex trial of white settlers, who were accused of murdering an Indian leader. The governor of the Northwest Territory appointed Tod as a special prosecutor and Edwards as one of the attorneys for the defendants. According to one account:

The trial attracted not alone all the settlers from up and down the river but from most remote parts. Great uneasiness prevailed and nerves were strained to the utmost for there was still fear of an outbreak among the Indians.[2]

Even though Edwards and his co-counsel won an acquittal for the defendants on the grounds of self-defense, the Indians in the area, agreeing that the trial was fair, accepted the verdict, avoiding further bloodshed.

In 1806, Edwards wrote a letter describing how far he and his fellow settlers had progressed since they first arrived:

We are but just well through the 4th of July. It was celebrated at Warren with great splendor. About one hundred citizens of Trumbull sat down to a superb dinner provided for the occasion. Seventeen toasts were drunk in flowing bumpers of wine under a discharge of fire-arms. The whole was concluded with a procession. . . .

You would have been surprised at the elegance and taste displayed on the occasion, recollecting that within seven years, on the same spot of ground, the only retreat from the heavens was a miserable log house, sixteen feet square, in which I was obliged to take my lodgings on the floor, wrapped in my blanket. . . . So much for New Connecticut. Do you think now we live in the woods, or is it surprising we forget that we do? The emigrations into this part of the country have been very large this spring. Mr. Tod is made a member of the supreme court of Ohio.[3]

Edwards was elected to Congress in 1813, but died before taking his seat, while George Tod was one of the first judges appointed to the Ohio Supreme Court. In 1806, he wrote a landmark opinion upholding a lower court's ruling that a law passed by the state legislature was unconstitutional. At the heart of the case was the question of whether Ohio courts had the authority to declare state laws unconstitutional.

It was ironic that ten years earlier, Tod had argued successfully against the principle of judicial review in a moot court proceeding at the law school. By taking the opposite position as a judge of the Ohio Supreme Court, Tod was tried for impeachment by the state legislature, but was acquitted by one vote. The result upheld in Ohio the principle of judicial review, which was established by the U.S. Supreme Court's 1803 opinion in the landmark case of *Marbury v. Madison*.[4]

In addition to Tod, two other law school alumni served as judges of the Ohio Supreme Court: John Crafts Wright (1831–1835) and William Virgil Peck (1859–1864; chief judge 1862–1863). After serving three terms in Congress, Wright was elected to the Ohio Supreme Court in 1831. Later, he moved from Steubenville to Cincinnati where he joined fellow alumnus, Edward King, as a founder of the Cincinnati Law School. Now called the Cincinnati College of Law, it is the most enduring of a number of law schools established by alumni.

The Wyoming Valley of Pennsylvania was also a preferred destination for law school alumni and their families who headed west from Connecticut and surrounding states. New England's rapidly growing population, along with the diminishing supply of arable land for farming, produced a continuous supply of customers for the land speculators.

Among the earliest of these emigrants was the family of future law school alumnus Noah Wadhams, who moved with his family from

Litchfield County to Wilkes-Barre, Pennsylvania, in 1773. In the same year, the Colony of Connecticut received royal approval to settle that region of Pennsylvania. That royal permit, however, conflicted with a prior royal grant of the same land to William Penn and his successors, leading to serious problems between the Pennsylvania and Connecticut settlers.

Following the Revolutionary War, armed conflicts continued in the Wyoming Valley between the disputing land claimants (called "Pennamites" and "Yankees"). In 1782, the two states asked the federal government to intervene, and a special court ruled in favor of Pennsylvania. However, it was not until 1799 that Connecticut finally relinquished all claims to land in the Wyoming Valley.

Putnam Catlin, who was born at Litchfield in 1764, read law with alumnus Uriah Tracy before moving in 1787 to Wilkes-Barre, the center of the Connecticut settlement in the Wyoming Valley. In 1794, the Luzerne County court minutes listed Catlin as the only attorney. The minutes also reported that alumnus Noah Wadhams, having been admitted to the bar in Connecticut, was "under the circumstances," admitted in Luzerne County.[5]

In 1817, Putnam Catlin sent his son, George, to study at the law school. Following his admission to the bar in Wilkes-Barre, George Catlin practiced law for only two years before he embarked on an artistic career and became one of the nation's most admired painters of Native Americans. As he later wrote:

> During this time, fortunately or unfortunately, another and stronger passion was getting the advantage of me. . . . After having covered nearly every inch of the lawyers table with penknife, pen and ink, and pencil sketches of judges,

jurors, and culprits, I very deliberately resolved to convert my law library into paint pots and brushes, and to pursue paint- ing as my future, and apparently more agreeable profession.[6]

As challenging as the pioneering life could be for law school alumni and their families in the backwoods of Ohio and Pennsylvania, it was an even more difficult experience for some who moved farther south and west. Silas Webster Robbins, a Yale graduate, studied at the law school in 1808. He and his wife, the youngest daughter of Uriah Tracy, moved to Kentucky, where he became a prominent lawyer and a judge on the Court of Appeals, the state's highest court.

During a financial crisis in the early 1820s, Kentucky's courts were widely accused of favoring the rights of creditors over debtors. Under political pressure, the legislature abolished the Court of Appeals and replaced it with a new court and judges. The "old court" judges, including Robbins, refused to recognize the "new court," and for sev- eral years there were two separate high courts, but eventually, the old court was reinstated.

Robbins later moved from Kentucky because he felt there was a "strong prejudice against Yankees." Settling in Springfield, Illinois, he became a leading member of the local bar and worked closely with Abraham Lincoln on many cases. Robbins defended himself in a case brought by a plaintiff who was represented by Lincoln. The ruling by the trial court in favor of Robbins was upheld by the Illinois Supreme Court on appeal, but Lincoln at least received ten dollars for his legal services.[7]

In another case, Robbins and Lincoln were co-counsel for two defendants who were sued as guarantors of a note when the debtor defaulted on the payments. A Lincoln biographer wrote that although

Lincoln and Robbins lost the case, it "illustrates the difficulty fron-
tiersmen had in finding cash and the role lawyers played in collecting
notes as substitutes for cash. . . . The lawyers on the Eighth Judicial
Circuit were the necessary agents to make trade possible."[8]

Lincoln was a self-taught lawyer without a college education,
while Robbins was a graduate of Yale, an alumnus of the Litchfield
Law School, and former Supreme Court judge. Yet both of them
achieved great success and professional standing in Springfield, which,
like most areas of the frontier, rewarded lawyers for skills and results
rather than backgrounds.

Two law school alumni, William Hull and William Woodbridge,
played prominent roles in the early years of Michigan as a territory
and state. When the Michigan Territory was created by Congress in
1805, President Thomas Jefferson appointed Hull, one of Tapping
Reeve's first students, as the territory's governor.

A territorial governor, like a British colonial governor before him,
was commander-in-chief of the militia forces, appointed the magis-
trates, held power over the judiciary, and conducted relations with the
Indians. At the outbreak of the War of 1812, President James Madison
prevailed upon a reluctant Hull, then sixty years old, to take command
of the Army of the Northwest. (Details of Hull's unfortunate fate in
carrying out his orders are described in Chapter Eighteen).

William Woodbridge, who attended the law school in 1802,
had a successful legal and political career in Ohio before moving to
Michigan in 1824 to become secretary of the Michigan Territory.
Woodbridge was elected governor of the new state in 1839 and two
years later was elected to the United States Senate. Among the many
testimonials included in a biography of Woodbridge, this best indicates
his many accomplishments:

But it is not solely our purpose to speak of him as an able lawyer. He has won laurels in the councils of his country, and whether advocating the claims of our infant Territory in Congress, or enforcing our rights to our soil . . . or opposing in our Legislature the aggressions of power . . . in all and each, he has evinced that fearlessness and independence, that stern regard for the best interests of his country; commanding talents combined with personal dignity, and a high sense of duty, which constituted him the chief ornament of our State.[9]

Real estate speculation in all the territories and new states attracted many lawyers around the turn of the nineteenth century. Their legal skills were needed to deal with deeds and titles and the frequent litigation which arose in areas of rapid development. Starting as lawyers or agents for speculators often opened opportunities for them to enter land speculation on their own.

One lawyer who was particularly successful in combining the skills of a lawyer and land speculator was Chester Ashley, who attended the law school in 1814. He then went west and practiced in Illinois before moving to the Missouri Territory, where he worked as a lawyer for the largest land speculator in the region. Ashley then settled in Little Rock in the Arkansas Territory and became the leading lawyer in land litigation cases, building the largest law practice in the state.

According to an Arkansas historical source:

His career was not spotless. . . . He was continually accused of fraudulent land speculation and behind-the-scenes political manipulation. . . . Despite these flaws, he was a consummate litigator . . . and participated in more appeals before the Arkansas Territorial Superior Court than any other attorney. In 1844, Ashley was elected to fill a vacancy in the U.S. Senate where he served as Chairman of the Senate Judiciary Committee until his death in 1848.[10]

It may have been Chester Ashley who recommended that George Claiborne Watkins attend the law school in 1833, its final year of operation. After Watkins returned to Little Rock and was admitted to the bar, Ashley brought his fellow law school alumnus into his firm as a partner. Watkins entered state politics in 1848 when he was elected attorney general of Arkansas and was later appointed by the legislature as chief justice of the state supreme court.

After the Civil War, Watkins formed a new partnership with Uriah M. Rose, through which the current Rose Law Firm in Little Rock traces its origin to the partnership of Ashley and Watkins. The firm's current legal specialties, ranging from "antitrust" to "intellectual property," are in stark contrast with the legal services provided by its pioneering ancestors.[11]

Daniel J. Boorstin wrote in one of his classic works:

When Judge Tapping Reeve lectured to the first law students in America at Litchfield, Connecticut, he gave his students the substance of Blackstone. Now reposing in the Yale Law Library, are sets of his students' lecture notes, yellow with age and worn from much use. These notes were carried west to Ohio to comprise the law library of the frontier practitioner. In this way, Blackstone's work, copied in the handwriting of American law students, was diffused throughout the west and was to help provide a foundation of legal ideas for the American hinterland.[12]

Chapter 11
The Deep South

Harvard historian Perry Miller wrote of the "amazing rise, within three or four decades, of the legal profession from its chaotic conditions of around 1790 to a position of political and intellectual domination." In the early decades after the Revolution, however, there was not enough work beyond land conveyancing and debt collection to support an increasing pool of lawyers in many of the new states.[1]

The legal profession's plight in Connecticut was summed up succinctly by a law student in the New Haven office of Simeon Baldwin (father of Roger Sherman Baldwin), who wrote in 1789: "The State of Connecticut was overstocked with lawyers."[2]

The Litchfield Historical Society's records indicate that roughly one-third of the more than three hundred law school students who were Connecticut residents at the time of enrollment moved elsewhere sometime after completing their studies. Dozens of the alumni went west, but a large number headed south, especially to Georgia and South Carolina.[3]

It is likely that some of those alumni were motivated to move south because of associations and friendships they made among the many southern students at the law school who shared their values.

More than twenty-five percent of all the known law school students came from the South, led by Georgia, which sent the fourth largest number of students between 1798 and 1817 and trailed only Connecticut and New York thereafter.[4]

Mark Boonshoft concluded from his research that many of the Southerners who attended the law school between 1805 and 1824 supported a national rather than regional agenda, especially in Georgia, but

> as the 1820s progressed, economic recession and escalating fears about slavery led many of these southerners to shed their nationalistic ideals, turn inward and embrace localism. At the same time, southern enrollment at the law school declined, though not completely.[5]

Another attraction of Georgia was the impressive record of achievements by many of the law school alumni, as noted by historian Thomas R. Hunter:

> There were seventy-one students who were either born in Georgia, or lived in the state at the time of their admission, not to mention at least eleven additional alumni who would later move to the state. These students form a veritable Who's Who of Georgia in the first half of the nineteenth century, including three members of the United States Senate ... thirteen members of the U.S. House and thirty-one state legislators.[6]

The first law school alumnus from Georgia to serve in the U.S. Senate was Nicholas Ware (1821 to 1824), who was previously mayor of Augusta. Ware is one of four alumni for whom Georgia counties are named. The other counties are named for John C. Calhoun (a South Carolinian), Stephen Upson, and William Crosby Dawson.

Among Dawson's achievements as a U.S. Senator was his championing of Henry Clay's attempt to avert a crisis between North and South. He helped to gain Daniel Webster's support for Clay when Webster, known as the "Great Orator," gave a famous speech in the Senate on March 7, 1850, in behalf of the Compromise of 1850, which began:

> Mr. President, I wish to speak today, not as a Massachusetts man, nor as a Northern man, but as an American, and a member of the Senate of the United States. . . . I speak for the preservation of the Union. Hear me for my cause.

Webster was widely attacked by abolitionists, including alumnus Horace Mann.

With the exception of the twentieth congressional session there was at least one law school alumnus representing Georgia in the U.S. House of Representatives from 1813 to 1841. The "dean" of the Georgia delegation was Alfred Cuthbert, who served nine years as a U.S. Representative followed by eight years as a U.S. Senator.

Cuthbert played a leading role in seeing that the federal government carried out the treaty with the Cherokee nation, which was promoted by President Andrew Jackson but passed the Senate by only one vote in 1838. It allowed a period of two years for the Cherokees to relocate before commencement of their forcible removal, known as the "Trail of Tears."

In one notable session of Congress (1839–1841), Cuthbert was one of five alumni (including John C. Calhoun) serving in the Senate, together with eleven alumni in the House, of which two were Georgians (William Crosby Dawson and Eugenius Aristedes Nisbet).

After serving one term in Congress, Nisbet was appointed by the Georgia legislature as one of the first justices of the Georgia Supreme Court when it was established in 1845. It must have been gratifying for him to be following in the judicial footsteps of his mentors, Judges Reeve and Gould, whom he called "the best law instructors in the Union."[7]

One admiring description of Judge Nisbet's influence on the development of jurisprudence in Georgia and beyond stated that:

> Eugenius A. Nisbet easily excels all his compeers as a perspicuous and polished expositor of the law, in its principles and precedents. The writers of the text-books, the judges of other courts, and . . . annotators . . . indulge in frequent quotations from his decisions . . . , and although his opinions are not ornate, yet the simple elegance and rhetorical finish of his opinions were doubtless largely due to his literary taste and culture.[8]

Nisbet's changing party allegiances over his long public career indicate the turbulent politics that prevailed in the state prior to the Civil War. When he served in the Georgia legislature in the late 1820s, he was a member of the States Rights Party. During his two terms in Congress he was a Whig, but in the 1850s he became a supporter of the nativist "Know-Nothing" or American Party. Although an ardent Unionist until the election of Lincoln in 1860, he introduced the resolution calling for disunion at the Georgia Secession Convention, in January of 1861.[9]

Another Georgia alumnus who had a long and distinguished career of public service was John C. Nicholl, a graduate of Princeton, who studied at the law school in 1814. After returning to his hometown of Savannah, he became mayor before serving as a federal judge for the state of Georgia between 1839 and 1861. Like Nisbet, Nicholl was a Unionist, but following Georgia's secession, he resigned from the federal bench and became the Confederate States attorney for Georgia until his death in 1863.

Of the dozen or more alumni who moved to Georgia after attending the law school, one of the most notable was William Tracy Gould, eldest child of James and Sally Tracy Gould. After graduating from Yale in 1816, he studied for three years at the law school, finishing just prior to the retirement of Tapping Reeve.

Rather than remain in Connecticut and, possibly, prepare to succeed his father at the law school, he moved to Georgia and settled in Augusta, the state's second-largest city (after Savannah) at the time. There he formed a partnership in 1823 with a fellow law school alumnus, Roger Wolcott Cooke, who was also a native of Litchfield. According to Thomas Hunter, Augusta was home over the years to at least eight natives of Litchfield and eleven alumni of the law school.[10]

Cooke died in a shipwreck shortly after the firm began, and Gould's younger brother, James Reeve Gould, died only three years after moving to Augusta from Litchfield to join his brother's firm. Despite these personal and professional blows, William Gould gained a statewide reputation as a skilled lawyer and legal scholar by the early 1830s.

In the same period, the health of his father had deteriorated to the point that he ceased lecturing and then made the decision to close the law school in 1833. That year, William Tracy Gould began lecturing to law students in Augusta. Perhaps he delayed the new venture in order not to compete for students with the Litchfield Law School. One of his initial class of students was Augustus Romaldus Wright, a future member of both the U.S. and Confederate congresses, who had studied at the law school in Litchfield in its final year.

When the Augusta Law School celebrated its first anniversary, William Gould stated in a published address:

> The institution is founded upon the same principle, and is, properly speaking a branch of the Litchfield Law School, Connecticut. The same lectures which were delivered there by James Gould are now delivered in the Augusta Law School by . . . Wm. Tracy Gould, except that instead of interspersing in the lectures information about the practice of Connecticut, information about "the Georgia practice" has been substituted.[11]

In making a case for his independent proprietary law school, Gould made it clear that "Law is not a science to be taught, as a part, merely, of collegiate education. . . . In order to make such schools suitable places of preparation for the bar, they should stand alone, unshackled by mere academic restraints."[12]

Gould managed to continue his law school for most of seventeen years, during which he educated more than one hundred fifty students. There were a number of factors that contributed to Gould's continuing success, including the lower transportation cost for students and the popularity of Gould as a teacher.

In Hunter's view, the primary reason was because

> Litchfield had always been extremely popular among Georgians, so, after its closure, the opportunity to stay within Georgia, yet receive an almost identical legal education—not only under the direction of the son of Litchfield's long-time proprietor, but also one that was especially geared toward practice in Georgia—undoubtedly proved irresistible.[13]

Another significant factor was the growing conflict between northerners and southerners over slavery, which had been far from resolved by the Missouri Compromise of 1820. Southerners who attended Harvard Law School were outnumbered by abolitionists, and as a recent history of the law school notes:

> As early as 1846, John Langdon Sibley, the abolitionist college librarian, had remarked in his journal: "The curse of the college is the Law Students, particularly from the South and Southwest States. . . . The effects of slavery are very perceptible in their deportment and immorality." Fist fights between Southern law students and the undergraduates were notorious.[14]

Among the best known of the Georgia (Litchfield) alumni was Augustus Baldwin Longstreet, whose most significant achievements were in the literary, publishing, and educational fields. Born in Augusta, he graduated from Yale and studied law at Litchfield in 1813, following in the footsteps of his older friend and role model, John C. Calhoun. Returning to Georgia, he practiced law, served as a judge, and was elected to the state legislature, all by the age of thirty-two.

After abandoning law and politics, Longstreet became a Methodist minister and temperance leader as well as a newspaper publisher and a college president (Emory College in Georgia, Centenary College in Louisiana, the University of Mississippi, and the University of South Carolina). Despite his success in each of these endeavors, he is probably best known as the author of *Georgia Scenes* (1835), a book one critic described as "a rich, hearty and imaginative description of rural and small town life in Georgia."[15]

One of the characters in the book was based on Longstreet's close friend and fellow alumnus, Edmund Bacon, who was a successful lawyer first in Georgia and then in South Carolina. Bacon became the senior partner and mentor of another alumnus, William Dickinson Martin, who was one of five South Carolina alumni that served in the U.S. House of Representatives. The others were John Campbell, John Felder, Eldred Simkins, and John C. Calhoun. The South Carolina alumni in the House, though fewer in number than their Georgia colleagues, compiled a longer record of continuous service—from 1811 to 1845.

Calhoun's political career began in 1808 when he was elected to the South Carolina legislature at the age of twenty-six. Following his service as a U.S. Representative (1811–1817), he served as secretary of war in President James Monroe's cabinet. He was initially a candidate for president in the election of 1824 but was elected as John Quincy Adams's vice president instead. In the election of 1828, he switched his allegiance to Andrew Jackson and won election as vice president for a second time. His illustrious career (detailed in later chapters) also included two long periods in the U.S. Senate, separated by a brief period as secretary of state.

It is worth noting one episode, known as the "Cumming-McDuffie duels," which exemplifies the close connection that existed among various alumni residents of Georgia and South Carolina in both their personal and professional lives. In 1822, Calhoun was competing with William C. Crawford of Georgia for southern votes in the upcoming presidential election. Longstreet and Calhoun were long-time supporters of George McDuffie, a South Carolinian who had recently succeeded alumnus Eldred Simkins, in the U.S. Congress.

Perceived insults and a challenge led to McDuffie having three duels with William Clay Cumming, a Georgian who was a contemporary of Calhoun's at the law school. Cumming, a supporter of Crawford and a hero in the War of 1812, had turned down an offer to represent Georgia in the U.S. Senate. In the course of the duels, McDuffie was seriously wounded but recovered and went on to become governor of South Carolina. Cumming survived unscathed and, according to one account, "preferred to live the life of a gentleman of leisure at his Augusta home."[16]

Cumming was one of eleven alumni who fought duels between 1804 and 1855 (a twelfth was settled at the last minute). Noting the death in a duel of one alumnus, *The Litchfield Ledger* observed:

> The death of Henry George Nixon caused the Legislature of South Carolina to pass severe laws against the practice of dueling. The custom was so deeply imbedded in the social structure of that day, however, that for a long time, these laws were dead letters on the statute books.

Interestingly, more of the dueling alumni were residents of New York than any other state or territory, with the most famous (or infamous) being Aaron Burr, who killed Alexander Hamilton in 1804. Incensed by that duel and Hamilton's death, Tapping Reeve's good friend, Lyman Beecher, delivered an anti-dueling sermon that was published in 1806 and widely read. It included this passage:

> Dueling is a great national sin. With the exception of a small section of the Union, the whole land is defiled with blood. From the lakes of the North to the plains of Georgia is heard the voice of lamentation and woe—the cries of the widow and fatherless. This work of desolation is performed often by men in office, by the appointed guardians of life and liberty. On the floor of Congress challenges have been threatened, if not given. . . . Alas! it is too late to conceal our infamy.[17]

Chapter 12

New York City

Hundreds of law school alumni migrated to the South and West from their home states, but New York was the only Mid-Atlantic state to attract a large number of alumni migrants. Between 1800 and 1850, the Mid-Atlantic region included three of the country's most populous cities (New York City, Philadelphia, and Baltimore). New York City was then, as now, a magnet for talented and ambitious people, but *The Litchfield Ledger* records list only twelve alumni who resided in Baltimore and nineteen in Philadelphia.[1]

Following the War of 1812, New York City experienced renewed economic growth, especially in banking and finance, along with more than enough lawyers needed to keep the wheels of commerce advancing. According to the Nile's Register of June 27, 1818:

> Lawyers are as plentiful as blackberries. From a late census of the New York Bar, it appears there are 1,200 attorneys and counsellors at law that are fostered in the bosom of the State [and] 290 are practicing in New York City.[2]

Like their counterparts elsewhere in the country, the great majority of lawyers in New York City did not attend law school until late in the nineteenth century. New York University started a short-lived law school in 1835, but Columbia Law School did not begin until 1858. Theodore Dwight, Columbia's first law school dean, acknowledged at the school's outset that most of the leading lawyers, who had obtained their training in law offices, were highly skeptical that professional schools could provide competent legal training.

Among the prominent New York City alumni of the Litchfield Law School was Charles H. Ruggles, who studied at the law school in 1803 but did not attend college. Because of his long public service as a state legislator, member of Congress, and trial court judge, he headed a committee to create a new judicial system when New York State held a Constitutional Convention in 1846.

His leadership at the convention earned him a seat in 1847 on the newly formed court of appeals, where he served for six years, including two years as chief judge. (In most states, members of the highest court are called justices of the supreme court, but in New York they are called judges of the court of appeals.)

One of Ruggles's most significant decisions was in the case of *Thomas v. Winchester*, which dealt with a mislabeled bottle of poison that was purchased from a druggist on a doctor's prescription. When taken by his patient, she became very sick and sued the manufacturer for damages, alleging negligence in mislabeling the bottle. The manufacturer lost in the trial court and appealed the decision to the Court of Appeals.

Courts had long held that the seller's common law duty of care was only to the immediate purchaser. Ruggles, in affirming the judgment of the lower court, established an "imminent danger to human life" exception to the established common law doctrine. It eventually led to courts adopting the doctrine of strict liability for defective products. In the landmark case of *MacPherson v. Buick Motor Company*, decided by the New York of Appeals in 1916, Judge Benjamin Cardozo noted that "the foundations of this branch of the law [product liability], at least in this state, were laid in *Thomas v. Winchester . . .*"

Lewis B. Woodruff, a native of Litchfield, Connecticut, finished at the law school in 1830. He practiced law in New York City for many years and served as a trial court judge before being appointed to the Court of Appeals in 1868. Among his notable decisions was *King v. Talbot* (1869), a case that developed the "prudent investor" rule for trusts, in which he stated:

> My own judgment . . . and bearing in mind the nature of the office [of a trustee], its importance, and the considerations which alone induce men of suitable experience, capacity and responsibility to accept its usually thankless burden, is that the just and true rule is that the trustee is bound to employ such diligence and such prudence in the care and management, as in general, prudent men of discretion and intelligence in such matters employ in their own like affairs. . . . The preservation of the fund and the procurement of a just income therefrom are primary objects of the creation of the trust itself, and are to be primarily regarded.

Woodruff's opinion abandoned the former strict limitations on investments and gave trustees more discretion in deciding how to invest trust assets. The case increased the usefulness of trusts and enhanced the trust and investment business for New York banks and other professional trustees as well as their lawyers.[3]

In 1869, President Grant nominated Woodruff to the newly

organized United States Court of Appeals for the Second Circuit. As it
does today, that court decided appeals from the United States District
Courts in Connecticut, New York, and Vermont. Woodruff was sworn
in as a federal judge in January 1870, and won high praise during his
six-year tenure on that court for his mastery of the rules of federal pro-
cedure and the special fields of admiralty, patent, and revenue laws.

Although Woodruff spent his professional life in New York, he
returned frequently to Litchfield. In 1870, he bought Tapping Reeve's
home as a summer residence and died there in 1875. When members
of the Bar of New York City met that year to honor Judge Woodruff,
one of the speakers remarked:

> His library was select, but, until he became a judge, it
> was not extensive, the main elements in it being "Gould's Lec-
> tures," in six volumes, copied by himself; and, whenever he
> had occasion to refer to authorities, those lectures were his
> principal assistance.[4]

A former law partner recalled:

> We formed a partnership about May, 1842. That con-
> nection continued with Mr. Woodruff until his elevation to
> the Bench in 1850 . . . and it was the connection of Mr.
> [Daniel] Lord and himself with the case of *Ogden v. Astor*
> which gave the former so high an estimate of Mr. Woodruff's
> abilities, and caused the promotion of Mr. Woodruff to the
> Bench, for I think that Mr. Lord was the active agent in hav-
> ing his name brought before the nominating convention.

Daniel Lord, Jr., one of the most prominent lawyers in the country prior to the Civil War, was born in 1795 and graduated from Yale with honors in 1814. After a year at the law school, he studied in New York City with another alumnus, George Griffin. As his own practice grew, Lord attracted many prominent clients, including John Jacob Astor, who had built his fortune initially as a fur trader.

In 1826, Astor sued a ship owner for damages caused by rats to some bear skins which he had shipped in one of the defendant's vessels from New Orleans to New York. Lord won the case for the ship owner on the grounds that rats were "perils of the sea." Astor was impressed by Lord's legal skills and thereafter retained him as his principal lawyer.

Astor greatly increased his fortune through real estate speculation. In 1809, he paid one hundred thousand dollars for future rights to the fifty-one-thousand-acre Putnam County estate of Robert Morris, a Tory who had fled to England. When Morris's widow died in 1825, Astor lost no time in taking ownership of the property and sending eviction notices to the hundreds of tenant farmers who lived on the estate.

The resulting uproar led to a series of lawsuits. The case against Astor, who was represented by Lord and a team of skilled attorneys, ultimately reached the U.S. Supreme Court, which found in Astor's favor. Finally, in 1830, Astor consented to sell the property to the state for five hundred and twenty thousand dollars.[5]

Astor was also criticized for his lack of philanthropy by many people, including alumnus Horace Mann, who wrote an article calling him "insane" for not giving back more to the community. With the advice of Lord and others, Astor eventually did provide for a gift in his will of four hundred thousand dollars to found the Astor Library, which was later incorporated into the New York Public Library. When

Astor died in 1848, Lord received substantial fees as an executor and attorney for the estate of the wealthiest person in the country.

The firm that Lord started in 1817 was renamed Lord, Day & Lord in 1845, recognizing the partnership he had formed with his son, Daniel De Forest Lord, and his son-in-law, Henry Day. The firm continued under that name for nearly one hundred fifty more years, but, after an unsuccessful merger, it closed in 1994, a victim of the rapidly changing economic conditions in the legal profession.

Another eminent New York City alumnus, Augustus Schell, combined political talents with legal skills. While building a reputation as an early expert in the new field of corporate law, Schell headed the State Democratic Committee for twenty years. In 1857, President James Buchanan appointed him collector of the port of New York, a position that was a prize plum of federal patronage, adding to Schell's influence.

After the scandal and downfall of William ("Boss") Tweed, Schell reorganized Tammany Hall and succeeded Tweed as the leader, called the "Grand Sachem." In the 1870s, Schell also served as chairman of the National Democratic Committee, but despite his vast political power, he ran unsuccessfully for both mayor and state senator.

Early in his political career, Schell became a close friend of Cornelius Vanderbilt, helping him expand his control of various railroads both as legal counsel and as a key member of numerous corporate boards. Following Schell's death in 1884, one of the many memorials stated:

> Augustus Schell early manifested the generous ambition which is the index of ability in youth. He pursued his preliminary studies with due diligence, and graduated with

marked distinction from Union College, in 1830, at the age
of eighteen. Devoting himself to the profession of the law, he
pursued his studies at that well-known institution in Connecticut, the Litchfield Law School—famous as the training-
school of many of the most eminent lawyers and
judges—under the direction of the late Judge Gould. . . .

Mr. Schell's ability as a lawyer, and wisdom in the
control and direction of great corporate interests, were early
recognized among the greatest of those men who have organized and wielded the gigantic power of successful enterprise
in developing the resources of the entire continent, opening
the great ways of communication through its vast territories,
and providing transportation for the products of America to
the markets of the world.[6]

By the middle of the nineteenth century, New York City was the
undisputed financial and commercial capital of the country. One book,
The Old Merchants of New York City, lionized the mid-century merchant princes of railroads, shipping, importing, retailing, finance, and
various other commercial ventures. The author, a journalist named
Walter Barrett, included this back-handed compliment to New York
City's leading commercial lawyers of the era:

A glorious occupation on this continent is that of a
merchant. . . . There is no class of citizens that excel, or even
equal him. . . . Lawyers are respectable, if they conduct their
business properly; but in this community they rarely raise
their heads, unless so lucky as to become patronized by merchants. Take Daniel Lord, Jr., the late George Griffin or

George Wood, Charles O'Connor, Francis B. Cutting, Francis R. Tilyon, John H. Power, James T. Brady, or Lewis B. Woodruff, or Charles P. Daly. Would these men, however great may be their abilities, ever have risen to the distinction they have reached, unless they had received the patronage and confidence of merchants? No. They are all rich. Would they have become so, but for the business afforded by merchants? No.[7]

Of the ten prominent lawyers cited by Barrett, four were law school alumni, including Lord, Griffin, and Woodruff. The fourth member of Barrett's legal pantheon, Francis B. Cutting, was a graduate of Columbia who studied at the law school in 1823. Like the others, Cutting developed a reputation for exceptional skill in the newly emerging field of commercial law. As one frequently quoted biographical note observed: "During fifteen years, from 1840 to 1855, there were very few cases tried in the metropolis involving questions of commercial law in which Mr. Cutting was not retained as the leading counsel on one side."[8]

Cutting is best remembered for his role in the "Great India Rubber Case," in which he, along with the famous Boston lawyer Rufus Choate, represented Horace Day, who was accused of infringing the vulcanization patents of Charles Goodyear. Representing Goodyear's interests was the renowned lawyer and statesman Daniel Webster, who took a two-week leave of absence from his duties as secretary of state to try what turned out to be his last major case. The court ruled against Day, but the trial drew nationwide attention not only because it involved such noted lawyers but because there was a fascination with new products in an era of new inventions.

Nathan Sanford had one of the longest and most distinguished public service careers of any alumnus during the early nineteenth century. After studying at the law school in 1798, he began practicing law in New York City and was selected at a young age as United States Attorney for the statewide District of New York. He resigned the position in 1815 when he was elected to the first of two separate terms as a U.S. senator.

In 1823, Sanford was appointed chancellor of New York, succeeding the illustrious Chancellor James Kent, who had reached the constitutionally mandated retirement age. Prior to the creation of the position of the chief judge of the New York Court of Appeals in 1847, the chancellor was the highest judicial officer in the state and headed New York's judicial system. In the 1824 presidential election, Henry Clay chose Sanford as his running mate, while John C. Calhoun was the vice-presidential choice of both Andrew Jackson and John Quincy Adams. Two years later, Sanford was re-elected to the United States Senate and resigned the chancellorship.

Like Nathan Sanford, Frederick A. Tallmadge spent much of his adult life in various political roles. Born in Litchfield, he was the son of Colonel Benjamin Tallmadge, the famous Revolutionary War spy master. Graduating from Yale in 1811, Tallmadge went directly to the law school and then served during the War of 1812 with a company of cavalry.

After the war, he settled in New York City, and embarked on a career that alternated between his law practice and politics. In addition to serving on the city's Board of Aldermen and as a member of the New York State Senate, Tallmadge was elected to the U.S. Congress in 1847 for one term. He was also appointed several times by the governor as the city's recorder, a position roughly similar to deputy mayor.

His most challenging role was as general superintendent of New York City's Metropolitan Police, which he assumed in 1857. This newly created position was part of an effort by the state legislature to take control of the New York City police force away from the mayor, Fernando Wood, and to fire many corrupt members of the force.

Those actions resulted in a battle, called the "Great Police Riot," which occurred in front of New York City Hall between the recently dissolved New York Municipal Police and the newly formed Metropolitan Police on June 16, 1857. Tallmadge was well qualified to lead the Metropolitan Police for five years during this difficult period because of his successful handling of the Astor Place Riots of 1849 when he was recorder.

His leadership of the Metropolitan Police may have served as a model for Theodore Roosevelt when he was Commissioner of Police a generation later. Similarities between the two men appear in the obituary of Tallmadge, published in the *New York Times* on September 18, 1869:

> Mr. Tallmadge was possessed of great moral as well as physical courage, and to mental abilities of a high order were added genial and polished manners. Although frequently obliged, from his position, to exercise power which was calculated to arouse bitter feeling, he always acted fearlessly but discreetly, and in such a way that he seldom made an enemy, and was deservedly popular with the masses.

Chapter 13

Upstate New York

I n addition to the nearly one hundred alumni who resided in New York City, hundreds of other New York State alumni were spread over numerous upstate communities from Buffalo in the west to Watertown in the north and Troy in the east. Many of these alumni continued their migrations, but a large majority stayed within New York State, even if they changed locations.

Lois Kimball Mathews's seminal work, *The Expansion of New England*, provides valuable insights into what led so many alumni to leave New England to settle in New York and farther west. In her view, after the early hunters, trappers, and poor farmers moved on, they were followed by

the third and best class of pioneers,—those who were young, ambitious and had a little capital with which to buy a farm and rear a family. . . . To the new home the young man brought his bride, and together they saved and planned and toiled till the log cabin was replaced by a substantial house, barns clustered about the home-lot, and from this group of buildings stretched away the acres of wheat and corn.

The farmer's chief desire at this stage was to raise more

than enough produce for his immediate needs; the surplus he sold, and the profits he invested in new lands about his home-farm. It is this class which brings the church, the school, the town meeting; this class which dreams of a college which shall reproduce Harvard, Yale, or Dartmouth; this class which aims at a seat in the legislature or the gubernatorial chair.[1]

Along with this "best class" of pioneering farmers came the merchants, bankers, and lawyers that the new farming communities needed to expand and achieve their "manifest destiny." The Western Reserve and Pennsylvania attracted many of the adventurous alumni, but proximity to their New England origins and families convinced many alumni that New York had more to offer. To many, upstate New York was "Greater New England."

Although Albany was one of the country's ten largest cities in the early nineteenth century as well as the state capital, Troy attracted the largest number of the alumni who settled in upstate New York. John Bird, a native of Litchfield and a Yale graduate, moved there shortly after finishing his studies at the law school in 1791.

A visitor to the small village of Troy in 1792 wrote: "There were from fifteen to twenty stores of all descriptions; several from two to four stories high. . . . The population of Troy at that time must have been several hundred and the surrounding country must have been thickly populated to support such a number of stores and taverns.[2]

Troy and the surrounding area benefited greatly from its location near the headwaters of the navigable Hudson River, allowing larger ships to sail to and from New York City. Its site on the east bank of the river also facilitated trade with communities throughout western New England. In 1802, John Bird was one of the founders of a company that constructed a turnpike to Schenectady in order to attract trade from the farmers residing west of the Hudson.

Although Bird was successful in his law practice and in politics, serving as both a state legislator and as a U.S. representative, he was less successful in his marriage. In 1797, his wife left him and took their two young children back to her family's home in Connecticut, where she was granted a divorce. Tapping Reeve, who was a member of the Connecticut court that ruled in favor of the former Mrs. Bird, noted in his treatise on domestic relations:

> It has been held, that if a husband turns his wife out of doors, and so abuses her, that she cannot live with him safely, and she departs from him; that this is not a willful absence on her part, but that it is so on his.[3]

Following the death of John Bird, who had remained in Troy, his ex-wife successfully sued the executors of his will in Connecticut for payment of child support. However, she was unsuccessful when she sued in New York to collect from Bird's estate on the judgment. Reflecting the differing common law principles that evolved among various states, the New York court held:

> The judgment in Connecticut was illegal and unjust. An action does not lie to compel a father to maintain and educate his child. The law cannot coerce a parent to do more than to keep his child from becoming a charge on the town.[4]

Bird was the first of thirty-three alumni who represented New York in the U. S Congress (three in the Senate and thirty in the House of Representatives). More than half of them were originally from New England.

One of the native New Yorkers was Barent Gardenier, who was born in Kinderhook, a town first settled by the Dutch around 1640. It was best known as the birthplace of President Martin Van Buren, whose nickname, the "Red Fox of Kinderhook," described both his red hair and his political cunning. The very brash Gardenier was described by the son of Josiah Quincy, a fellow member of Congress:

> Among the new friends of Mr. Quincy . . . was Barent Gardenier, of New York, a self-made, self-educated man, of fiery temperament, reckless courage, and fluent speech. My father had a warmly affectionate regard for him, and loved to tell of his sayings and doings. He says of him in a letter to my mother: "He is a man of wit and desultory reading, accustomed to the skirmishing and electioneering violence of New York. He brings it all into debate in an honest, unguarded, inconsiderate manner, very well calculated to inflame the party passions opposed to him, but not to make converts; but, withal, he is an excellent fellow."[5]

After studying at the law school in 1796, Gardenier practiced law in Kingston, New York, and was also editor and publisher of a Federalist newspaper, the *New York Courier*. In the election of 1806, Gardenier was elected to Congress as a Federalist and was reelected in 1808, distinguishing himself as a noted orator.

His strong views on many political issues caused frequent conflict with some of his fellow politicians, especially with Congressman George Washington Campbell of Tennessee. Campbell charged Gardenier with "falsehood, meanness and baseness" in stating that the House was governed by French influence.

The disagreement became so heated that Gardenier challenged Campbell to a duel, which subsequently took place on the infamous dueling field in Bladensburg, Maryland. Gardenier was seriously wounded, but he recovered, and his constituents reelected him to his second term. Campbell went on to enjoy a distinguished career as a senator, secretary of the treasury, and minister to Russia.

Another Connecticut native, Samuel Miles Hopkins, left the law school in 1791 and started practicing law in the then remote village of Oxford in south central New York. In a memoir, he described the challenges of practicing law on the state's western frontier:

> My first law draft I made by writing on the head of a barrel, under a roof made of poles only, and in the rain, which I partially kept from spattering my paper by a broad brimmed hat. . . . The first case I ever tried was in defending a man indicted for forgery, which was death, and on which the attorney general of the State in person supported the prosecution. Judge Hobart sustained the objection I took, and the prisoner was acquitted. And in this country I rode 80 miles to Newtown (Elmira) to attend a Court of Common Pleas in my own county, and was too happy to win a jury case and get a fee of $8, perhaps the most gratifying I ever received. Sometimes I rode all day in the rain, forded the swift flowing Chenango in water up to my horse's back, found my whole library and stationery wet by the operation and lost my way

in returning up the river, the path—not road—being too
blind to follow.[6]

Like many other law school alumni, Hopkins combined his legal
practice with politics, but he reversed the usual progression, serving
first as a member of Congress and later in the state legislature at Albany
in the 1820s. During his service in both houses of the legislature, a
major issue was the construction and funding of the Erie Canal.

Begun in 1817 and completed in 1825, the canal linked the
waters of Lake Erie in the west to the Hudson River in the east. From
its opening days, countless numbers of pioneers took advantage of the
new inland waterway and its faster, safer, and smoother mode of travel.
A daughter of Hopkins wrote of her family's experience in traveling
on the canal:

> In 1832 it was decided that we should remove to Geneva,
> in order that my father might spend his last days near his much-
> loved sister Mrs. Dwight. We made the canal journey on board
> a new packet-boat chartered for the occasion, the forerunner,
> though we dreamed it not, of the modern house-boat. This was
> our home for a week; the cabin was a pleasant parlor, with
> piano, center table, books, games and work; and it was an expe-
> rience which we would gladly have prolonged; but it was ended
> by our arrival at our pleasant home in Geneva. [7]

Some of the most successful of the upstate New York alumni
settled in towns and cities along the Erie Canal. Troy, near its eastern
terminus, had become very prosperous by the time George Gould
arrived there in 1830, shortly after finishing his law studies with his

father, James Gould. Adding to his success as a lawyer and businessman, Gould was elected mayor of Troy before serving as a judge for eight years.

Roughly one hundred fifty miles to the west of Troy, Syracuse was also benefiting from the canal traffic of goods and people when alumnus Elias Leavenworth settled there in 1827. The law firm that he founded was one of the most successful in the state and paved the way for his success as a politician, first as mayor of Syracuse and later as a U.S. representative.

Timothy Childs, who studied at the law school in 1814, was one of the earliest of the alumni to settle in Rochester, which was another major beneficiary of the Erie Canal. Both Childs and Frederick Whittlesey, who was at the law school in 1819, turned their prominence as Rochester lawyers into successful political careers as local leaders of the Anti-Masonic Party.

Strongly opposed to Freemasonry, the party emerged as a political force in the late 1820s, originally in western New York. It grew out of the mysterious kidnapping and presumed murder of a man named William Morgan, who had published an exposé of the Masonic order. The party's adherents believed that Freemasonry was a corrupt and elitist secret society that controlled too much political power locally and nationally.

According to one account, "the anti-Masonic fury raged around Rochester as its center, and Timothy Childs was twice elected to Congress from this district as an anti-Mason." For a brief period, the Anti-Masons became an important third-party alternative to Jackson's Democrats and Adams's National Republicans. In New York, the Anti-Masons even supplanted the National Republicans as the primary opposition to the Democrats. Like Childs, Whittlesey was elected to Congress on the Anti-Masonic ticket.[8]

The movement spread beyond New York, and in 1832 alumnus

Darius Lyman was narrowly defeated when he ran for governor of Ohio as a member of the Anti-Masonic Party. Also that year, the party's candidate for vice president, Amos Ellmaker of Lancaster, Pennsylvania, lost to John C. Calhoun, who was a year ahead of him at the law school. Most of the Anti-Masonic Party's members became Whigs in the 1830s, and the party disappeared after 1838. In the view of one historian: "Politically, Anti-masonry's greatest achievements were introducing the nominating convention to presidential politics and contributing to the development of the Whig party."[9]

The principal promoter of the Erie Canal was DeWitt Clinton, who was governor of New York when the canal was completed in 1825. His son, George W. Clinton, was a student at the law school in 1828 and moved to Buffalo in 1836. Just two years later he was appointed collector of customs for the port of Buffalo by President Van Buren, thereby benefiting directly from the canal that had once been called "Clinton's Folly." He was mayor of Buffalo from 1842 to 1844 but served for twenty-three years as judge of the superior court, including the last seven years as chief judge.

Like Clinton and four other upstate alumni who entered New York politics as mayors, Daniel S. Dickinson served as the original president (mayor) of Binghamton at age thirty-four. He went on to have a distinguished political career as a state senator, lieutenant governor, and U.S. senator. Dickinson then practiced law for a decade until returning to public office as the state attorney general in 1861.

Prior to the Civil War, Dickinson was one of the state's most prominent proponents of southern states' rights, and, in 1860, he hoped to be selected as the compromise presidential candidate at the Democratic National Convention. Dickinson was described by one historian as

[A] fearless and unceasing opponent to the demands of political radicalism of the period. But in many ways he was a radical, for his States' Rights proclivities were a little too strong, his adherence to the Constitution a little too unyielding, his expansionist ideas a little too greedy, and his gift of oratory a little too overpowering.[10]

One other upstate New York alumnus deserves mention for a variety of reasons, including his memorable name, Augustus Cincinnatus Hand. Born in Shoreham, Vermont, he moved across Lake Champlain to Elizabethtown, New York, in the Adirondacks after finishing his studies at the law school in 1828.

He remained there until his death in 1878, developing a flourishing legal practice and serving as a state senator, member of the U.S. House of Representatives, justice of the state supreme court and, briefly, as a judge on the New York Court of Appeals.

His legal legacy was continued by his three sons, who all became lawyers, as well as by two of his grandsons. One of those grandsons, Learned Hand, distinguished himself during thirty years as a trial and appellate judge through his qualities as a judge and his writing skills. Many legal scholars consider him one of the greatest American judges.

A biographer of Learned Hand wrote that he grew up on tales of his grandfather, "the rebellious farm boy who somehow, by 'hook and crook,' God knows how, managed to get down to Judge Gould's law school in Litchfield, and who, because he was very industrious and had great competence, achieved much."[11]

The same could be said for many of the law school alumni, both the college graduates and the farm boys.

Chapter 14

New England

The colonial Provinces of New York and New Hampshire maintained a bitter conflict for decades over territory known as the New Hampshire Grants. When New York's claims finally received the necessary royal support, it began to evict many of the settlers in an effort to gain control of the region. The settlers, in turn, resisted the "Yorkers" by forming a militia named the "Green Mountain Boys," commanded by the legendary folk hero Ethan Allen.

The long-running dispute was largely resolved when the area named Vermont (originally called New Connecticut) was established as an independent republic in 1777. However, continuing objections from New York over settlement of conflicting property claims kept Congress from granting the independent Vermont Republic admission to the union until 1791.

One of the leaders of Vermont's long campaign for statehood was Stephen Row Bradley, who moved there from Connecticut in 1779 after studying law with Tapping Reeve and serving with distinction in the Connecticut militia during the war. A Vermont historian described Bradley as a "prominent political leader, who exercised a large influence in laying the foundation of the state of Vermont."[1]

After the admission of Vermont into the union, Bradley was elected as one of the state's original U.S. senators and represented his adopted state in the senate with distinction for more than fourteen years, as described in Chapter Eighteen.

Bradley's early political success may have been due in part to his close association with the highly popular Ethan Allen as both his friend and lawyer, despite their vastly different personalities. A Yale graduate, Bradley was cultured and intellectual while Allen, a farmer's son from Litchfield County in Connecticut, was rough-hewn and flamboyant. Yet, as one of Allen's biographers noted: "While it is true that he was not distinguished for modesty or refinement, it should be borne in mind that the New Hampshire Grants was not a region well suited to the cultivation of the graces and adornments of life."[2]

Bradley was the first of ten alumni (all but one of them from Connecticut) who rose to important political and judicial positions after moving to Vermont. One of the most prominent was Richard Skinner, another native of Litchfield, who attended the law school in 1798 and moved shortly thereafter to Manchester, Vermont.

His twelve years as a state attorney and probate judge provided sufficient political connections and name recognition for him to win elections to both the state legislature and the U.S. Congress. Beginning in 1820, he was also elected by wide margins to three successive terms as governor.

Rounding out his distinguished career, Skinner was chosen as chief justice of the Vermont Supreme Court in 1823 and served until 1829, when he retired from public life for good. He died in1853, from injuries caused by being thrown from his carriage while crossing the Green Mountains.

Horatio Seymour's career was remarkably similar to Skinner's, beginning with their origins in Litchfield, where they were born in May of 1778 to mothers who were relatives. While Seymour and Skinner both studied at the law school in 1798, Seymour graduated from Yale, but Skinner did not attend college. He was one of a number of students who were accepted by Reeve and Gould because of future potential, rather than past education.

After settling in different Vermont communities in 1800, Skinner and Seymour, like many other alumni, began their political careers by serving as the state attorney in their home counties. In 1820, each of them reached the pinnacle of their political careers when Skinner was elected to his first term as governor while Seymour was selected for a seat in the U.S. Senate, where he served for twelve years.

A third Vermont leader, Samuel S. Phelps, was also a native of Litchfield and an alumnus of its law school. He was described by one Vermont historian as:

> Senator for thirteen years, councilor, Supreme Court judge, and one of the ablest and most accomplished men the state has ever had in public life, [he]was born at Litchfield, Conn, in May, 1793, of a family that had for generations been one of intelligent well-to-do farmers. Litchfield was in those days a breeding ground for able and influential men, and has probably turned out more than any town of its size in the country. It then contained the very best law school in the country. The intellectual friction of such associations was of incalculable benefit for such a bright youth as Phelps, and here may be found the foundation of his greatness.[3]

Although fifty former law school students chose to live in Vermont, only twelve alumni settled in New Hampshire, even though its population exceeded Vermont's for most of the period between 1800 and 1850. Despite their small number, three of the alumni were counted among the most distinguished civic leaders of the "Granite State." James Bell, Jared Warner Williams, and Levi Woodbury all became U.S. senators, and the latter two also served as governors.

To those achievements, Woodbury added service on the state supreme court, cabinet positions in both the Jackson and Van Buren administrations, and, most significantly, six years as an associate justice of the U.S. Supreme Court (aspects of his federal service are described in later chapters).

A native of a small town in New Hampshire, Woodbury graduated from Dartmouth and studied at the law school in 1809. After returning to his native state, he rapidly built a successful law practice as well as a reputation for intellect and hard work. During his service as clerk of the state senate in 1816, his talents so impressed the governor that he appointed Woodbury as an associate justice of the state's supreme court at the age of twenty-seven (he was nicknamed the "baby judge").

The majority of the court decided in an important case that Dartmouth should be governed by a new public board of trustees rather than according to its state-approved private charter. That decision was appealed to the U.S. Supreme Court, which ruled in favor of the college's independent trustees in a landmark decision. Their attorney and Dartmouth alumnus, Daniel Webster, argued successfully that abrogating Dartmouth's charter violated the federal constitution's protection for the sanctity of contracts and stated that:

You may destroy this little institution. . . . But, if you do so, you must carry through your work! You must extinguish, one after another, all those great lights of science, which, for more than a century have thrown their radiance over our land![4]

In addition to the seven alumni from Vermont and New Hampshire who served in the U.S. Senate, there were five Massachusetts alumni who were members of the House of Representatives. Alumnus Peleg Sprague, who spent much of his life in Massachusetts, was elected to both the U.S. House and Senate from Maine.

A graduate of Harvard, Sprague attended the law school in 1813 and soon afterward moved to Maine, which was then a district of Massachusetts. He became politically active in the movement to gain statehood for Maine, a long-sought goal that was finally achieved in 1820 as part of the Missouri Compromise.

After leaving the Senate in 1835, Sprague moved to Boston to practice law and was appointed in 1842 as judge of the U.S. District Court in Massachusetts. While serving on that court for more than twenty years, he lost his sight completely but could still perform his judicial duties because of his prodigious memory.

In a tribute to Judge Sprague, the noted author and lawyer Richard Henry Dana, Jr., wrote in 1864, just prior to Sprague's retirement from the bench:

It is not generally known that the magistrate commonly called the United States District Judge has the most varied, and in some respects the highest jurisdiction ever exercised by a single judge in England or America. In the District

Court, he tries alone causes of admiralty jurisdiction, of whatever amount, all revenue causes, whether in admiralty or at
common law, and all criminal causes, under the Federal jurisdiction. . . .

But the District Judge is also *ex officio* Circuit Judge. . . .
He can try causes of equity, patents, copyrights, and all common law causes within Federal jurisdiction, questions of pre-
rogative writs, and all criminal causes; and from his single
decision on the law in a trial even for murder, piracy or treason, there is no appeal. This has been the jurisdiction and
these the functions which your fellow citizen, Judge Sprague,
has exercised for the last twenty years, a great magistrate and
an incorruptible man.[5]

Two other Massachusetts alumni, Theron Metcalf and Marcus
Morton, served for many years on the Massachusetts Supreme Court.
Morton wrote that court's opinion in *Charles River Bridge v. Warren
Bridge,* a famous case that eventually went to the U.S. Supreme Court.
The plaintiff company, which owned a toll bridge constructed in 1786,
claimed it had been granted a monopoly that was infringed when a
competing bridge enterprise was issued a state charter in 1828.

In his opinion, Morton ruled that if the state intended to grant
an exclusive right to the plaintiffs, it had to do so explicitly. This
reasoning was upheld in 1837 by the U.S. Supreme Court in an opinion written by Chief Justice Taney with a concurrence by Associate
Justice Baldwin, who was nine years ahead of Morton at the law school.

Morton maintained an active political career in the years when
he was not on the bench, serving as governor of Massachusetts three
times. During his term as the state's first Democratic governor in 1839,

Morton was unsuccessful in opposing the plan of educational reformer and fellow alumnus Horace Mann, which called for greater state control over education.[6]

When he served in Congress in the early 1820s, Morton was a close friend of fellow alumnus John C. Calhoun, but, by the1830s, he had distanced himself from Calhoun and the southern wing of the Democratic Party over slavery. Yet his relationship with Calhoun survived well enough for Morton to seek his aid in gaining approval from southern senators in 1846 for his appointment as collector of the port of Boston. In a letter to Calhoun, Morton wrote:

> I admit at the outset that I am *opposed,* (if you please) *decidedly opposed* to slavery. But I deny most emphatically that in any way I ever did anything to aid or encourage the abolition party or the doctrine of abolition.[7]

Morton's plea succeeded, and he held the plum port collector's position for four years.

The most extraordinary chapter in Morton's political career began in 1842 when he was reelected governor, winning by one vote over his Whig opponent. A major factor in Morton's victory was his support for the goals of a populist uprising in the neighboring state of Rhode Island, led by a lawyer named Thomas Wilson Dorr, which became known as the "Dorr Rebellion."

At the time, Rhode Island was among the few states that did not provide broad suffrage for white males, which had resulted in the control of state government by rural residents and large land-owning interests. Among the governing elite were two law school alumni, Moses Ives Brown (Dorr's brother-in-law) and Richard Ware Greene, the State's attorney general, who later served as chief justice of the state's supreme court.

When Dorr and his followers failed in an attempt to seize the state arsenal in Providence, martial law was declared. The rebellion rapidly collapsed, and Dorr fled the state with a bounty on his head. Upon his return to Rhode Island in 1844, he was arrested and tried. The court consisted of four justices of the state supreme court, including alumnus George A. Brayton. Brayton had joined the court in 1843 and remained until his resignation in 1874, serving the last six years as chief justice.

On June 20, 1844, Dorr was sentenced to life imprisonment in solitary confinement. Governor Marcus Morton came from Massachusetts to speak at a large rally in Providence, urging Dorr's release. His speech helped to increase the public outcry, which gained freedom for Dorr in 1845.

In the view of one historian, the Dorr Rebellion could have been avoided if moderate members of the governing elite, like law school alumnus John Brown Francis, had prevailed. Francis was an influential former governor, who later served in the U.S. Senate, but the state's conservative leaders resisted reform until it was too late.[8]

Like Rhode Island, which waited until 1843 to adopt a constitution, Connecticut continued to rely on its colonial charter until 1818. A tradition of continuity in the leadership of its governmental, social, and religious institutions led to the state being called the "Land of Steady Habits."

Chapter Eight ("Fading Federalists") describes some of the clashes between leaders of the Federalists and Jeffersonian Republicans in Litchfield and other parts of Connecticut. These led to major political and societal changes, especially in the aftermath of the War of 1812. In the view of historian Wesley W. Horton:

If the Republicans were going to dislodge the Federalists,
their best alternative was to advocate a new constitution . . .
the Republicans eventually succeeded, politically and constitutionally, because they were on the winning side of three
issues: religious freedom, separation of powers and expanded
suffrage.[9]

In 1817, law school alumnus Oliver Wolcott, Jr., (a former Federalist and Congregationalist) led a new coalition, called the Toleration
Party, in winning the gubernatorial election as well as control of the
state legislature. The Toleration party was a fusion of former Federalists
and Republicans as well as Episcopalians, Congregationalists, and other
denominations, whose principal goal was to secure religious freedom
in Connecticut.

The political success of the reformers paved the way for holding
a constitutional convention in 1818, chaired by Oliver Wolcott.
Among the delegates were a number of other alumni, including
Nathan Smith, a close political ally of Wolcott's, who was later elected
a U.S. senator. When the proposed constitution was submitted to the
Connecticut voters for ratification, it was approved by a simple majority of only 1,554 votes out of a total of 26,282.[10]

Nonetheless, Wolcott and his colleagues in the legislature were
able to enact numerous legislative reforms with relatively little opposition during his ten years as governor that ended in 1827. Wolcott's
distinguished public service career spanned more than fifty years,
beginning in 1795 when he succeeded Alexander Hamilton as treasury
secretary.

Another alumnus, Henry W. Edwards, capitalized on family
connections as well as political skills during his long career in public

service, which culminated in five years as governor in the 1830s. He was the grandson of the renowned theologian Jonathan Edwards and son of Pierpont Edwards, a leading Connecticut lawyer and judge, who was a political ally of Thomas Jefferson.

In April 1802, Pierpont Edwards wrote to President Jefferson:

> I . . . request that my son, Henry Waggaman Edwards . . . may be appointed as one of the [bankruptcy] commissioners for this district—he is well known to the Vice President [Aaron Burr, who was Henry's cousin] . . . [11]

Three months later, the young Edwards (then age twenty-four) was appointed a bankruptcy commissioner. It was the first of many positions he held in a long political career, which included service in both houses of the state legislature as well as in the U.S. Senate and House of Representatives.

In 1833 Edwards, a Democrat, was elected governor but was defeated the following year by fellow alumnus Samuel A. Foot, a Whig. Re-elected governor in another contest with Foot in 1835, Edwards served until 1838. He was succeeded that year by another alumnus, William W. Ellsworth.

Like Levi Woodbury of Vermont and Marcus Morton of Massachusetts, Ellsworth had successful careers in the legal, judicial, and political worlds. After studying at the law school in 1811, he practiced law in Hartford and was appointed as the first law professor at Trinity College.

When Ellsworth joined the Connecticut Supreme Court as an associate justice in 1847, alumnus Samuel Church had just become chief justice, succeeding Thomas S. Williams, who had retired after eighteen years on the court. Between 1806 and 1874, nine alumni served on the Connecticut Supreme Court, of whom three were chief justice.

When Chief Justice Williams died in 1861, one of his colleagues observed:

> He brought to the bench a very unusual combination of qualifications peculiarly fitting him for the station. He well understood that the law as a practical science, could not take notice of melting lines, nice discriminations and evanescent quantities. . . . Metaphysical refinements and hair-splitting distinctions had little influence with him. In his decisions, he was exceedingly impartial. He ever looked at the case, and not at the parties. It may, I think, with great truth be asserted, that he had no respect of persons in judgment. He heard the small as well as the great.[12]

Considering the large number of students (more than 300) who entered the law school from Connecticut, it is not surprising that so many of them contributed significantly to the governance and welfare of that state, including eight who became U.S. senators and twenty-four who served in the U.S. House of Representatives. However, it is noteworthy how many more of the Connecticut alumni who migrated north, west, and south made similar contributions to their adopted states and territories. Later chapters will describe the influence that many of them had at the national level.

Chapter 15
Business and Commerce

The *Ledger*, maintained by the Litchfield Historical Society, provides online biographical information for nearly one thousand known alumni in many categories, including their professions, which for the great majority is listed simply as "lawyer." In many cases, however, alumni combined other work with the practice of law in order to support their families and achieve their own personal and financial goals.

In addition, a substantial number of alumni either never practiced law, or left the legal profession to pursue careers in business, commerce, and other fields. In each capacity, they helped the country develop from a largely agricultural base to a more diversified economy while contributing to the expansion of investment and banking opportunities.

A notable example is alumnus James Bell, a New Hampshire lawyer, who later served as a U.S. senator. He successfully negotiated between the small landowners of the New Hampshire lakes region and powerful mill companies that depended on the water power of the Merrimac River for their operations. His success in obtaining the riparian rights for leading manufacturers assured the continued growth of mills in Massachusetts and New Hampshire.

As alumni migrated across the country, the law school's reputation for training superior lawyers helped many of them gain clients and professional recognition. Some of the most valuable clients were real estate investors, who needed laws researched, documents drafted, and disputes resolved or litigated. A number of the alumni continued to practice law while acting as land agents or investors.

Among the earliest to combine his law practice with land speculation was Samuel A. Law, who became a land agent in Western Pennsylvania in the 1790s. So many settlers from his hometown of Cheshire, Connecticut, were attracted to the area by him that they named a town Lawsville in his honor. Like many other lawyers of the period, Law was also a farmer.

As mentioned in Chapter Ten, John Starke Edwards moved in 1799 to the Western Reserve of Connecticut as an agent for his father, who was a principal investor in the Connecticut Land Company. Among the other investors were two alumni—Uriel Holmes, Jr., and Uriah Tracy—and the fathers of six other alumni. Established in 1795, the Connecticut Land Company bought a large portion of the territory that later became Ohio.

Despite its short existence and financial problems, the company was instrumental in the development of the region, including the settlement of Cleveland, named for Moses Cleaveland, a principal partner in the Connecticut Land Company. The city's name was supposedly contracted by an editor because it did not fit in a headline.

Another ambitious land venture involved alumnus Stephen Cleaveland (no relation to Moses). He was one of the organizers in 1834 of the Trinity Land Company that aimed to colonize an area near the Trinity River in Texas prior to the war with Mexico. With the assistance of their land agent, Sam Houston, they acquired roughly six hundred twenty thousand acres from the Mexican government.

The partners, in turn, sold scrip (certificates) to individual subscribers, authorizing them to take possession of undefined parcels of
land. This scheme, which enriched Cleaveland and his New York partners, created a "bubble," inflating land values in anticipation of Texas
gaining independence from Mexico.[1]

Cleaveland was wise not to join the seventy men, women, and
children who sailed from New York to Galveston Bay in the spring of
1834. After landing in Texas, the colonists had to travel more than one
hundred miles up the Trinity River to locate their farming tracts. The
remote wilderness area and coastal fevers discouraged most of the pioneers, and by the fall, only nine of them remained. It was one of the
hazards for pioneers in opening up the frontier of the country.[2]

One of the most successful of the alumni real estate investors was
Alexander N. Fullerton, a native of Vermont and graduate of Middle-
bury College. After attending the law school in 1826, he initially practiced law in Troy, New York. When he moved to Chicago in 1833, it
had a population of about two hundred fifty but was growing rapidly.
That year he joined with other community leaders to incorporate the
small settlement as a town.

As one of the founding fathers and a talented investor, Fullerton
amassed a vast fortune in Chicago real estate as well as Michigan lum-
bering enterprises. Fullerton Avenue, Chicago's longest street, was
named for him, as was Fullerton Park and the Fullerton River.

Fullerton may have moved from Troy to Chicago because he had
seen the great success and could envision the future potential of the
Erie Canal, which was completed in 1825. The canal was not only substantially increasing business for New York City, it was helping the
growth of communities in upstate New York from Troy to Buffalo and
beyond. One historian observed:

Now pioneering farmers in the West could ship their grain, lumber, and salted pork through frontier lake ports like Detroit, all the way to New York. And New York could transship them almost anywhere in the world with its magnificent merchant ships, which were still powered by wind in the sails. The canal that helped make New York the country's busiest saltwater port would soon make Chicago the country's busiest freshwater port.[3]

Alumnus Junius Smith was among the first entrepreneurs to see the potential for innovating transatlantic shipping by using steam engines. After studying at the law school in 1802, his law practice in New Haven took him to London, where he lived for many years. Frustrated by the slow passages on sailing ships between England and America, he formed a company in 1836 to build a prototype steamship. Surmounting numerous problems of funding and delays, he achieved his initial goal, but eventually his company was overtaken by competitors like Cunard. Nonetheless, Junius Smith is seen by many as a pioneer in the modernization of ocean shipping.

In 1843, Smith closed the company and returned to the United States. He established a plantation in Greenville, South Carolina, called Golden Grove, and made an unsuccessful attempt to establish a commercial tea plantation. His anti-slavery sentiments led to a brutal beating by his neighbors in 1851, from which he never fully recovered. He died in the Bloomingdale Asylum in New York in 1853.

Not long after leaving the law school in 1824, John Lloyd Stephens abandoned a career as a lawyer, initially becoming a well-known traveler and writer. In 1839, President Van Buren appointed him as special ambassador to the Federal Republic of Central America, which led to his writing about the rediscovery of the Mayan civilization.

Like Junius Smith, Stephens became a major promoter of steam navigation as a sponsor of the Ocean Steam Navigation Company. Shifting his interest to railroads, Stephens helped to establish the Panama Railroad Company, which became the first commercial link between the Atlantic and Pacific on the Isthmus of Panama when it was opened in 1855.

The public and commercial interest in building canals was eclipsed by the rapid development of railroads, beginning in the 1820s. One of the earliest successful lines was the Philadelphia and Columbia Railroad, which was built in lieu of a canal. When it was chartered by the Pennsylvania legislature in 1826, alumnus Amos Ellmaker of Harrisburg was appointed one of the original directors. Ellmaker was also a director of the Pennsylvania Railroad, which absorbed many lines, including one linking Philadelphia, Wilmington, and Baltimore, and whose initial management included two Baltimore alumni, John Charles Groome and James Wilson Wallace.

In 1828, alumnus Andrew DeWitt Bruyn was appointed by the New York legislature as a director of the Ithaca and Owego Railroad Company, the fourth railroad in the state. It connected the town of Ithaca, on the southern shore of Cayuga Lake, with the town of Owego, on the Susquehanna River to the south. The railroad provided a link connecting the Erie Canal and the Great Lakes to the coal fields of Pennsylvania and ports on Chesapeake Bay.

Unlike other alumni, whose involvement with railroads was largely incidental to their legal work, William P. Burrall became one of the country's leading railroad executives. After completing his studies at Litchfield in 1828, Burrall practiced law in the nearby town of

Canaan and became expert in the negotiation of railroad contracts. He played an instrumental role in the consolidation of many small lines into major corporations. Because of his executive abilities, he was selected president of the Illinois Central Railroad and, later, as president of the New Haven and Hartford Railroad, two major lines.

Coincidentally, Burrall was preceded as chief executive of both railroads by another alumnus, Robert Schuyler. A member of a distinguished family that was part of New York's Old Dutch ("Knickerbocker") aristocracy, Schuyler was a grandson of Philip Schuyler, a famous Revolutionary War general, and a nephew of Alexander Hamilton.

After graduating from Harvard, he studied at the law school in 1818, but gave up the practice of law to become an investment broker in New York City, specializing in railroad investments. He also became president of several major railroads and was known as "America's first railroad king."

While serving both as president and sole stock transfer agent of the New York and New Haven Railroad in the early 1850s, Schuyler issued unauthorized stock, worth two million dollars, which he sold for his personal gain and used as collateral on loans. It was the country's first large stock fraud and led to years of legal battles over the accountability of the railroad's directors.

When his brokerage firm failed in 1854, Schuyler borrowed six hundred thousand dollars from his good friend, Cornelius Vanderbilt, who ended up with the largest number of the bogus shares. Before a warrant for Schuyler's arrest was issued, he fled via Canada to Europe and died there in obscurity.

According to one account,

> Mr. Schuyler's course was the consequence of the diffi-
> culties in which he had involved himself in connection with
> the building of other railroads . . . where large sums had been
> sunk by the original subscribers. The discovery of the above
> frauds created a universal panic that for a while threatened to
> break up the railroad system throughout the country.[4]

Finally, in 1865, the New York Court of Appeals ruled that the
company was liable to the defrauded shareholders for the losses, which
amounted to nearly two million dollars. When investors approved the
consolidation of two lines into the New York, New Haven, and Hartford Railroad in 1872, appointment of the well-regarded William P.
Burrall as a senior executive helped to overcome the bitter memory of
Schuyler's fraud and win the support of investors.[5]

Another alumnus, James Gore King, who earned a sterling reputation as a private investment banker in New York City, was also an
early president of the New York and Erie Railroad. One account states
that

> he was largely instrumental in gaining for the railroad
> the confidence of the community, and in giving it an impulse
> toward its completion. Resigning this post during the finan-
> cial crisis of 1837, he went abroad, proved to the governors
> of the Bank of England the wisdom of helping American mer-
> chants, and induced them to send to this country, to assist
> the banks, £1,000,000 in gold—a large sum in those days—
> which they did through his [banking] house. The result was

that confidence was restored, the banks resumed specie payments, and the crisis was passed.[6]

King was a partner in several investment firms during his career, but the most prominent was Prime, Ward & King, whose first major financial success was in buying Erie Canal bonds and reselling them to clients. As the authors of the invaluable work *Gotham: A History of New York City to 1898*, describe:

> Among their best clients was the highly respected Baring Brothers firm of London. . . . In 1823, Barings bought their first Erie Canal bonds from Prime, Ward & King. Eager British investors snapped them up, and the Barings began to buy more, and by 1829, a majority of the Erie Canal debt was owned overseas. . . . Even during the runaway market of 1832-34, when the Barings curtailed their investments in anticipation of a crash, the house continued to deal with substantial firms in New York City, primarily Prime, Ward & King.[7]

Investment firms and private banks were allowed to operate as partnerships, but commercial banks had to be incorporated and receive a charter from the state legislature. The first commercial bank in New York City was the Bank of New York, founded in 1784 by Alexander Hamilton. It enjoyed a monopoly until 1799, when a group headed by alumnus Aaron Burr obtained a state charter for The Manhattan Company. Although its stated primary purpose was to supply fresh water to Manhattan residents to counter a yellow fever epidemic, the broad charter provisions allowed it also to conduct a commercial banking business. It has evolved over the years into J. P. Morgan Chase.

The New York Chemical Manufacturing Co. was founded to produce medicines, paints, and dyes at a plant in Greenwich Village, but, following the lead of The Manhattan Company, it later used its excess capital to open a bank. In 1844, the reorganized Chemical Bank appointed alumnus John Quentin Jones as president. When the country entered a severe depression in 1857, eighteen New York City banks closed in a single day. Chemical, however, was the only bank to redeem notes in gold instead of in loan certificates, giving the Bank its nickname of "Old Bullion."

A history of the Chemical Bank painted this picture of Jones:

> Mr. Jones's bachelor life, his dislike for ostentation, and his unremitting attention to the affairs of the Chemical Bank caused him, long before he could properly be termed old, to be styled a man of unusually methodical habits. It was, however, this strict adherence to business, combined with a rare judgment and sagacity in financial affairs, that enabled him to witness the growth of the Bank from a non-dividend paying institution in 1844, when he became its president, to one paying 100 per cent dividends, while the original one hundred-dollar shares had risen to a value of $1,600 shortly before his death.[8]

While New York City became the financial center of the country, Hartford earned the title of the nation's insurance capital. In the spring of 1819, a number of prominent Hartford businessmen, led by alumnus Thomas K. Brace, petitioned the Connecticut legislature to authorize the incorporation of the Aetna Insurance Company as a pioneer underwriter of fire insurance. The statute granting the charter noted that the name "Aetna" referred to the famous volcano on the east coast of Sicily, which, "though surrounded by flame and smoke, is itself never consumed." A year later, Aetna's board received approval for a charter amendment to permit the writing of life insurance and annuities. .

Brace, who has been called the "father" of American life insurance, served as the company's first president and remained on the Board of Directors until his death in 1860. He was succeeded as president by alumnus Henry Leavitt Ellsworth, whose twin brother, William Wolcott Ellsworth, served with him as a director as well as Aetna's first general counsel.

In addition to the alumni who passed up legal careers to develop land, improve transportation, finance projects, and insure against a growing number of risks, others became inventors as well as producers and marketers of various products. A notable example was Eli Whiney Blake, nephew of the inventor of the cotton gin, who studied at the law school in 1817.

Instead of pursuing a legal career, he joined his uncle in building and running a gun factory. After his uncle's death in 1825, Blake and two of his brothers continued to run the arms business until they started a new firm to capitalize on their engineering and entrepreneurial talents.

Under the name of Blake Brothers, the firm became a pioneer in the manufacture of door locks and latches. Gradually, its product line was expanded to include casters, hinges, and other articles of hardware, most of which were covered by their patents. In 1851, Blake invented a steam-powered rock crushing machine after watching workers crush stones with hand hammers for road construction. The patented machine, which was designed to crush stone into various sizes and shapes, revolutionized road-building, mining, and other industries.

Like Blake, Walter Baker joined a family manufacturing firm after finishing his law studies and became the head of the Baker Chocolate Company upon the retirement of his father in 1824. For almost thirty years Walter Baker expanded production and made Baker's Chocolate a recognizable name across the country. He was ahead of his time in emphasizing marketing and promoting good customer relations.

The Baker's Chocolate Company continued to make its best-selling chocolate and cocoa products in Dorchester, Massachusetts, long after the death of Walter Baker in 1852. General Foods, which purchased the company in 1927, finally closed the factory there in 1965 and moved it to Dover, Delaware, where it is now part of the Kraft Heinz Company.

Chapter 16

Supreme Court Justices

The nine justices currently on the U.S. Supreme Court are alumni of only three law schools: Harvard (4), Yale (4) and Columbia (1). Not surprisingly, more alumni of those prestigious law schools have served on the nation's highest court than alumni of any other law school: Harvard (20), Yale (11) and Columbia (7). It is remarkable, however, that next in number of alumni is Litchfield Law School, which is tied with Michigan Law School (3 each).[1]

In 1830, Henry Baldwin became the first Litchfield Law School alumnus to join the court as well as the first justice who had attended a law school. After graduating from Yale in 1797, Baldwin studied with Tapping Reeve and then moved to Philadelphia to continue his studies. His mentor was Alexander Dallas, a prominent attorney who also acted as the first reporter of decisions for the U.S. Supreme Court, which was then located in Philadelphia.[2]

Admitted to the bar in 1801, Baldwin moved to Pittsburgh and began to rise rapidly in both the legal profession and the Democratic-Republican (Jeffersonian) Party. Pittsburgh had a population of less than two thousand when Baldwin arrived, but steadily grew from a frontier town to a manufacturing center. He ran successfully in 1816 for a seat in the U.S. House of Representatives and advocated aggressively during his three terms in office for tariffs to protect his constituents' industrial interests.

Also, his effective defense in Congress of Andrew Jackson's controversial military tactics against the Native Americans in Florida during the first Seminole War earned Jackson's lasting support. Baldwin's health forced him to resign from Congress in 1822, but he continued to provide valuable political assistance to Jackson in the key state of Pennsylvania, helping him win the presidential election in 1828.

Baldwin was not offered a cabinet position as he had hoped, but he was rewarded in 1830 by Jackson, who nominated him for a seat on the Supreme Court. In a demonstration of bipartisan support, he was confirmed by the Senate in a vote of forty-one to two. Jackson had to dissuade Baldwin from resigning after his second year on the court over Baldwin's strong opposition to what he believed was the unconstitutional extension of the court's powers under the leadership of Chief Justice John Marshall.

After Jackson persuaded him to stay, Baldwin remained on the court for fourteen years. During his tenure, he tended to seek a middle ground between Marshall's expansive view of national power and the extreme positions taken by states' rights advocates. Although Baldwin is generally ignored or criticized by most legal scholars, the noted legal historian Charles Warren praised the "superb opinion" by Baldwin in the case of *United States v. Arredondo*:

Few decisions of the Court at this period had a more permanent effect upon the history of the country; for in this case the Court established the public land policy of the Government on the basis of the most scrupulous respect for treaties, preferring to preserve the honor, rather than the property of the government, and to run the risk of confirming possibly fraudulent claims rather than to impair the reputation of the Government with foreign nations.

Warren then noted:

> Consequently, the decisions of the Court upholding the claims were a great disappointment and gave grave offense to the President, so much so, that, as reported in the newspapers, he sent for Judge Baldwin, who drew up the opinion of the Court, and gave him a lecture. . . . As Baldwin was an appointee of Jackson, the episode forms another striking illustration of the independence of the Judiciary from Executive influence.[3]

Though highly praised for his indefatigable industry, integrity, and knowledge of the law, Baldwin nevertheless saw his reputation as a jurist tarnished by his independent spirit and eccentricity. It has been widely reported that Baldwin was frequently at odds with his fellow justices, and a number of Supreme Court historians have concluded that Justice Baldwin suffered from mental illness, including Mark Levin, who wrote:

> In 1832 it was reported that [Baldwin] "was seized today with a fit of derangement." Less than two weeks later, Daniel Webster alerted a friend to the "breaking out of Judge Baldwin's insanity," and another correspondent observed more pithily that "Judge Baldwin is out of his wits." Baldwin was hospitalized for what was called "incurable lunacy" and missed the entire 1833 term of Court. Joseph Story informed Circuit Judge Joseph

Hopkinson in May 1833 that, "I am sure he cannot be sane. And, indeed, the only charitable view, which I can take of any of his conduct is that he is partially deranged at all times."[4]

Baldwin also frustrated his fellow justices by dissenting in a number of cases, ignoring Marshall's strong preference for unanimous decisions. In the 1832 case of *Worcester v. Georgia*, he was the lone dissenter when the court held that the states had no power to interfere with the Cherokee people or their lands. President Jackson ignored the majority opinion and supported the forced removal of the Cherokees to western territory.

In the noted case of *United States v. The Amistad*, decided by the Supreme Court in 1841, Baldwin not only dissented but did not write an opinion explaining the reasons for his dissent. The case, nonetheless, had a special connection to the Litchfield Law School, because another alumnus, Roger S. Baldwin, was the lead counsel for the plaintiffs. Roger and Henry Baldwin had no close family relationship even though they both grew up in New Haven (Henry was thirteen years older), went to the same preparatory school, and graduated from Yale before studying at the Litchfield Law School.

The *Amistad* decision was one of the most significant among a number of slave cases heard by the Supreme Court prior to the *Dred Scott* decision. The case grew out of a revolt in 1839 by enslaved Africans on board the ship *Amistad*, which was sailing between two ports in Cuba. Some of the crew members were killed, but the survivors were ordered by the rebels to return the ship to Africa.

Instead, they sailed north until the ship was seized off the coast of Long Island by a U.S. revenue cutter. The Africans were arrested and jailed while a federal court dealt with the competing arguments of Spanish ship owners, purchasers, and others who claimed them as property.

Seeking to maintain good diplomatic relations with the Spanish government, President Van Buren ordered the U.S. district attorney in Connecticut, William S. Holabird (another alumnus), to charge the captives with murder and piracy. Roger Baldwin was persuaded by a group of fellow abolitionists to represent the African defendants.

At their trial in the Connecticut Federal District Court, Roger Baldwin argued effectively that the rebels were neither pirates nor slaves. The court ruled that no one owned the Africans because they had been illegally enslaved and transported to the New World. The Van Buren administration appealed the decision, and the case came before the U.S. Supreme Court in January 1841.

Former president John Quincy Adams was added as Baldwin's co-counsel on the appeal, but Baldwin delivered most of the arguments over more than a week of hearings before the Supreme Court. According to one account, "Known for his irascible temperament, Adams gave a bitter and sarcastic argument that stood in stark contrast to that of Baldwin, who addressed the international legal questions with reason and aplomb." The Court ruled in favor of freedom for the Africans in a seven-to-one decision, with the lone dissent coming from Henry Baldwin.[5]

Despite his continuing health problems, Baldwin remained on the court until his death in 1844. A year later, President James K. Polk's interim nomination of alumnus Levi Woodbury was confirmed by the Senate, and he joined the court in January 1846.

Woodbury had already served as governor of New Hampshire and associate justice of the state's supreme court as well as two separate terms as a U.S. senator. His political skills impressed Andrew Jackson, who appointed him to two cabinet positions, first as secretary of the navy and then as secretary of the treasury.

When Martin Van Buren succeeded Jackson as president, he

retained Woodbury as his treasury secretary. During his long tenure, he laid the foundation for a more independent treasury system and adroitly managed the department through the protracted battle over the national bank as well as the Panic of 1837.[6]

In his second year on the court, Woodbury wrote the majority opinion in a major slavery case (*Jones v. Van Zandt*), upholding the constitutionality of the Fugitive Slave Act of 1793. Although personally opposed to slavery, he stated that the framers of the Constitution had reached a problematic compromise on the issue of slavery, and that it was "a political question, to be settled by each State by itself."

Like Baldwin, Woodbury generally supported states' rights and opposed the extension of federal courts' powers and jurisdiction. His apparently pro-southern positions had allied him with fellow alumnus John C. Calhoun when they were both members of Jackson's cabinet. When Calhoun was considering a run for the presidency in the 1840s, Woodbury was a possible northern choice for his running mate.[7]

According to historian Timothy S. Huebner, Woodbury had his own presidential ambitions:

> Woodbury sometimes seemed more interested in the presidency than in his judicial post. Some historians speculate that his pro-South judicial record represented an effort on his part to position himself for the White House, and that, had he lived longer, he, rather than Franklin Pierce, New Hampshire's other leading Democrat, would have been nominated to run for president in 1852.[8]

Woodbury died in 1851, and it was not until 1873 that a third alumnus, Ward Hunt, was confirmed by the Senate as an associate justice of the Supreme Court. A life-long resident of Utica, New York, Hunt was chief judge of the New York Court of Appeals before New York's Republican boss, Roscoe Conkling, persuaded President Ulysses S. Grant to nominate Hunt for a seat on the Supreme Court.

Unlike Henry Baldwin, Hunt dissented in only seven cases during his ten years on the court, including *United States v. Reese* (1875). That case involved the question of whether Kentucky's voting inspectors were subject to criminal penalties for failing to accept the votes of males of African descent under the Fifteenth Amendment. Hunt disagreed with the majority opinion, which held that the indictment was technically flawed, thereby affirming the opinion of the lower courts. In his view, the ruling weakened the Enforcement Act of 1870 and impeded state implementation of the Fifteenth Amendment, which banned racial discrimination in voting.

Interestingly, Hunt is probably best remembered for another voting rights criminal case, in which he was the trial judge (part of the circuit court duties required of a Supreme Court justice at the time). The defendant was Susan B. Anthony, the women's suffrage crusader. She had been charged with voting in the 1872 federal election in violation of New York law and the state constitution, which did not permit women to vote.

During her trial, Anthony argued that the barring of her vote was an unconstitutional violation of the Fourteenth Amendment, but Hunt ordered the jury to enter a guilty verdict. In his decision, Hunt determined that the rights set forth in Amendments to the Federal Constitution were guaranteed to citizens of the United States, but not to citizens of the states. He therefore ruled that each state had the right to set its own voting qualifications. The next day, Anthony's attorney made a motion for a new trial, which Justice

Hunt denied. He then asked Anthony: "Has the prisoner anything to say why sentence shall not be pronounced?"

Anthony responded:

> Yes, your honor, I have many things to say; for in your ordered verdict of guilty, you have trampled underfoot every vital principle of our government. My natural rights, my civil rights, my political rights, my judicial rights, are all alike ignored. Robbed of the fundamental privilege of citizenship, I am degraded from the status of a citizen to that of a subject; and not only myself individually, but all of my sex, are, by your honor's verdict, doomed to political subjection under this, so-called, form of government.[9]

Despite Anthony's eloquent protestations, Hunt sentenced her to pay a fine of one hundred dollars plus the costs of prosecution, a penalty she refused to pay. There was no appeal by Anthony, but in 1875 the Supreme Court ruled, in a similar case (*Minor v. Happersett*), that female suffrage was not guaranteed by the Fourteenth Amendment or any other part of the Constitution. By then, the leaders of the women's suffrage movement had decided to pursue a non-judicial solution, which finally succeeded when the Nineteenth Amendment was ratified in 1920.

Because of a series of illnesses, Hunt's active participation on the Supreme Court lasted less than ten years. The general view is that his tenure on the court did not achieve the potential forecast by the *New York Times* when he was nominated: "No appointment which President Grant has made has been based upon stronger recommendations than that of Judge Ward Hunt to the Supreme Court of the United States."[10]

TAPPAN REEVE.

From a painting by George Catlin.

Engraving of Tapping Reeve by Peter Maverick.
Collection of the Litchfield Historical Society, Litchfield, Connecticut.

Pulling Down the Statue of King George III.
Engraving by John C. McRae. Library of Congress.

Aaron Burr.
Engraving by Enoch Gridley (1804). Courtesy of Yale University Art Gallery.

Litchfield Law School Museum building, present day.
Collection of the Litchfield Historical Society, Litchfield, Connecticut.

Litchfield Law School Museum interior, present day.
Collection of the Litchfield Historical Society, Litchfield, Connecticut.

Portrait of James Gould by Samuel Lovett Waldo (ca. 1803).
Courtesy of Yale University Art Gallery.

Vintage postcard image of James Gould's office at the Litchfield Law School.

Woodcut of William Grimes, artist unknown (1825).
From *Life of William Grimes, the Runaway Slave.*

Portrait of John C. Calhoun by Charles Bird King (ca. 1818).
Courtesy Chrysler Museum of Art, Gift of the Grandy family in memory of C. Wiley Grandy.

Portrait of Oliver Wolcott, Jr., by George Catlin (1827).
Collection of the Litchfield Historical Society, Litchfield, Connecticut.

Photograph of William Tracy Gould (ca. 1850).
Collection of the Litchfield Historical Society, Litchfield, Connecticut.

Portrait of William Hull by John Trumbull (1790).
Courtesy of Yale University Art Gallery.

Portrait of Peter Buell Porter by Daniel Huntington (1873).
The Picture Art Collection.

Portrait of Henry Baldwin by Thomas Sully (1834).
The Picture Art Collection.

Portrait of Levi Woodbury by Charles Fenderich (1837).
Lithograph on paper, National Portrait Gallery, Smithsonian Institution;
transfer from the Library of Congress.

Portrait of Sarah Pierce attributed to George Catlin (ca. 1825).
Collection of the Litchfield Historical Society, Litchfield, Connecticut.

Portrait of George Catlin by William Fisk (1849).
Courtesy of the National Portrait Gallery.

Portrait of Horace Mann by Francis D'Avignon (1859).
Lithograph with tint stone on paper. National Portrait Gallery, Smithsonian Institution.

Chapter 17

Nation's Service (1789–1807)

I t is striking how many Litchfield Law School alumni held prominent political positions at the national level, including one hundred U.S. representatives and twenty-eight U.S. senators. One or
more alumni participated in every session of Congress from 1791 to
1859 as well as in the sessions of 1861 to 1863 and 1877 to 1879.[1]

Although it is well known that Aaron Burr and John C. Calhoun
each became vice president, it is not as well known that Calhoun served
with two presidents of opposing parties: John Quincy Adams and
Andrew Jackson. Six alumni, who were members of presidential cabinets, headed a total of twelve departments in the nine administrations
of eight presidents:[2]

President	Alumnus	Department
Washington	Oliver Wolcott, Jr.	Treasury
Adams	Oliver Wolcott, Jr.	Treasury
Monroe	John C. Calhoun	War
Jackson (first)	Peter B. Porter	War
	Levi Woodbury	Navy
Jackson (second)	Levi Woodberry	Treasury
Van Buren	Levi Woodbury	Treasury
Tyler	John C. Calhoun	State
	John Y. Mason	Navy
Polk	John Y. Mason	Attorney General
	John Y. Mason	Navy
Taylor	John M. Clayton	State

Some historians have criticized Reeve and Gould for concentrating on private rather than public legal principles in their law school curriculum despite the public service contributions of so many alumni at the local, state, and federal levels. A noted legal historian, Paul D. Carrington, wrote:

> Those who taught law in American colleges before 1870 were seldom striving to prepare their students to perform legal services for private clients. . . . What they sought was to inculcate standards of public conduct appropriate to popular self-government subject to constitutional restraints. . . ,
>
> Harvard . . . was, perhaps, less clear about the mission. It had established a "law" school in 1815 to emulate the Litchfield Law School. . . . Reeve's program emphasized the study of private law and had little in common with the

initiative [at William and Mary] of Jefferson, whom Reeve reviled. Like Harvard, Yale at times, replicated Litchfield.[3]

Another legal scholar, Steve Sheppard, commented about the curriculum taught by Reeve and Gould:

> The course was rooted in the practicalities of the common law governing private disputes, skipping public law topics of Constitutional government and politics, Roman civil law and stately lectures on the great principles of the Law of Nature.[4]

By focusing only on the curriculum, these commentators ignore many other elements of the students' law school experience, which, in Carrington's words, helped to "inculcate standards of public conduct." Among the most important were the examples of public service set by earlier alumni, beginning with Aaron Burr and Stephen Row Bradley, who became members of the U.S. Senate in 1791.

There were numerous influential exemplars of public service in the Litchfield community, most notably Oliver Wolcott, Senior and Junior. George Washington made at least two visits to Litchfield during the 1780s, staying at the home of the senior Wolcott, who was both a Connecticut delegate to the Continental Congress and a Major General in the Connecticut militia.

A neighbor of Wolcott's, Elihu Hubbard Smith, recorded in his diary in September 1780: "It was this autumn, I suspect, that I first saw the illustrious Washington. Then too, and then only, I saw La Fayette, who was with him . . ."[5]

Oliver Wolcott, Jr., was educated at Yale and studied law with

Tapping Reeve in 1778. After gaining experience as the state comptroller in Connecticut, Wolcott served under Alexander Hamilton in the U.S. Treasury Department, first as auditor then as comptroller.

Upon Hamilton's resignation in January 1795, Wolcott succeeded him as secretary of the treasury and continued in the office during the administration of President John Adams until resigning in December 1800. Although Wolcott was generally praised for tight management of the nation's finances, he was a target of political attacks from supporters of Jefferson in Congress, because he was an ally of Hamilton.

In his biography of Alexander Hamilton, Ron Chernow describes Wolcott's difficult relationship with Adams:

At moments, however, Wolcott grew ambivalent about the idea of Hamilton exposing Adams, arguing that "people [already] believe that their president is crazy." In the end, though, convinced that Adams would ruin the government, Wolcott told Hamilton that "somebody had to write a few paragraphs exposing the folly" of those who had idealized Adams as a noble, independent spirit.[6]

Despite their apparent friction, Adams appointed Wolcott to a newly created seat on the United States Circuit Court for the Second Circuit in February 1801, just prior to leaving office. He was one of thirteen circuit court judges appointed to positions created by the Judiciary Act of 1801, which became known as the "Midnight Judges Act."

In the long period after Wolcott finished his studies with Reeve in 1778, he had little legal and no judicial experience. One historian noted:

In the decision to appoint Oliver Wolcott, personal or political motivations were obviously primary; both the President and the Connecticut Federalists preferred to take Wolcott and drop Jonathan Sturges, whose qualifications at bench and bar were far superior. Unabashed by the possible complications resulting from so unlearned a judge, the Senate approved the nomination and Wolcott received immediate congratulations from . . . Senator Uriah Tracy [his fellow alumnus and Litchfield neighbor].[7]

The most gratifying message must have been the one he received from Adams, who wrote Wolcott:

When the public discards or neglects talents and integrity, united with meritorious past services, it commits iniquity against itself by depriving itself of the benefit of future services, and it does wrong to the individual by depriving him of the reward which long and faithful services have merited. Twenty years of able and faithful service on the part of Mr. Wolcott, remunerated only by a simple subsistence, it appeared to me, constituted a claim upon the public which ought to be attended to.[8]

After all of the "midnight judges" positions were abolished by enactment of the Judiciary Act of 1802, Wolcott became a leader of an effort to have the Supreme Court rule that the 1802 Act was unconstitutional. He argued that the Constitution permitted revocation of federal judicial appointments only if there was evidence of bad behavior.

When attempts to obtain redress from both the Supreme Court

and Congress proved unsuccessful, Wolcott moved to New York to enter business and restore his finances. He eventually returned to his hometown of Litchfield and ran successfully for governor in 1817. Abandoning his Federalist roots, he headed the new Toleration Party, which forged important changes in state laws and practices through a long-delayed constitutional convention.

In histories of the period, the saga of the Midnight Judges Act is overshadowed by the dramatic contest between Thomas Jefferson and Aaron Burr in the presidential election of 1800. When the election ended, they both had the same number of electoral college votes, so the winner had to be decided by the House of Representatives.

The deadlock continued through thirty-five ballots in the House, while the Federalists, who held the deciding votes, debated which candidate to favor. According to a biographer of Burr, Hamilton wrote on December 17, 1800, to Wolcott "rebuking vehemently the proposal to elect Burr President by Federal votes."[9]

On the next ballot, a deal between Jefferson and some Federalists brought him the votes he needed for victory. As one historian noted:

> The mystery is not why Jefferson would deny making such an accord, but why he changed his mind after vowing never to bend. . . . Burr's behavior is more enigmatic. He had decided to make a play for the presidency, only apparently to refuse the very terms that would have guaranteed it to him. . . . It may have been that the Federalists demanded more of him than they did of Jefferson. Or Burr may have found it unpalatable to strike a bargain with ancient enemies, including the man he would kill in a duel three years later.[10]

To avoid a repetition of the 1800 election problem, Congress considered various solutions, which culminated in the proposed Twelfth Amendment to the Constitution. It provided that electors would continue to cast two votes, but one of the two votes would explicitly be to fill the presidency, while the other designated who should become vice president.

A principal drafter of the amendment was alumnus Stephen Rowe Bradley, a Republican senator from Vermont. Opposing the resolution was another alumnus, Senator Uriah Tracy, a staunch Federalist senator from Connecticut, who argued in a lengthy speech for preserving the original terms of the Constitution (Article II):

> I shall attempt to prove . . . that the resolution before us contains principles which have a manifest tendency to deprive the small States of an important right, secured to them by a solemn and Constitutional compact, and to vest an overwhelming power in the great States. And, further, I shall attempt to show that, in many other points the resolution is objectionable, and, for a variety of causes, ought not to be adopted.[11]

Nonetheless, the resolution was adopted by Congress and the amendment was ratified by the last of the requisite number of state legislatures on June 15, 1804.

During Jefferson's first term as president, Bradley, who was a close ally of Jefferson, served as president pro tempore of the Senate on occasions when Vice President Aaron Burr was absent from the chamber.

Burr was generally praised for his skill and fairness in presiding over the Senate, except in his role at the impeachment trial of Supreme

Court Justice Samuel Chase. His behavior was then likely due to the effects of his recent duel with Hamilton and his indictment in New York and New Jersey for murder.

Enough of the Republican majority in the Senate joined all of the Federalists to acquit Chase of the charges. As told by Robert Caro in his prize-winning biography of Lyndon Johnson, *Master of the Senate*:

> One Federalist, Uriah Tracy of Connecticut, ill with pneumonia, left his bed and was carried to his seat because Chase's supporters believed that every vote would be needed. They were wrong, as was shown by the very first vote cast by a Republican senator on the first article of impeachment. The vote, by Stephen Bradley of Vermont, was "Not guilty."[12]

Former Chief Justice Rehnquist observed:

> Chase's narrow escape from conviction exemplified how close the development of an independent judiciary came to being stultified. . . . The political precedent set by Chase's acquittal has governed that day to this: a judge's judicial acts may not serve as a basis for impeachment.[13]

Burr's political career continued in a downward spiral following the duel and death of Hamilton as well as Jefferson's decision to drop him as a running mate in the 1804 election. Three years later, Burr was arrested by order of Jefferson and charged with treason, allegedly for plotting to invade Mexican territory and create an independent nation in the Southwest. One historian, Nancy Isenberg, contends in her biography of Burr:

Burr never planned the grand conspiracy that attached to him, and neither did he seriously contemplate the assassination of the president or his own installation as emperor of Mexico (all things he was charged with at various points).[14]

Chief Justice John Marshall presided at the 1807 treason trial of Burr held in the Circuit Court for the District of Virginia at Richmond. According to Charles Warren, "No case of the day aroused more intense excitement or enlisted a more brilliant array of counsel . . ."[15]

Burr actively planned his defense strategy with his distinguished team of lawyers, which included two former U.S. attorneys general as well as leaders of the Maryland and Virginia Bars. During the proceedings, Jefferson kept in close contact from the White House with the equally talented team of prosecutors. The trial was the first major test of the Constitution's treason clause, which states in part:

> Treason against the United States, shall consist only in levying war against them, or in adhering to their enemies, giving them aid and comfort. No person shall be convicted of treason unless on the testimony of two witnesses to the same overt act, or on confession in open court.

At the trial, Marshall made the unusual move of issuing a subpoena to President Jefferson to deliver documents that Burr had requested to prepare his own defense. Jefferson only supplied parts of the letters to the court and never acknowledged the subpoena, claiming executive privilege. Burr's defense, however, depended on evidence that showed that Burr was one hundred miles away from the location where the government claimed Burr was planning an overt act of treason.

The jury deliberated only a short time before entering a verdict that Burr was not guilty of treason. Even then, Burr had to face additional charges claiming that he had violated the Neutrality Act. When the government could not introduce sufficient evidence that Burr had planned an invasion of Mexico or any other part of New Spain, he again won a verdict of not guilty.

As one chronicler of the trials observed:

With that decision . . . the crowds began to disperse. The defense team disbanded, and the prosecutors faded out of the limelight. The jurors had gone and the witnesses all went on their ways. The trial of the century had ended.[16]

Chapter 18
Nation's Service (1808–1825)

In 1807, President Jefferson persuaded Congress to enact a trade embargo against Britain and France, which worsened economic conditions in many parts of the nation but especially in New York and New England. In a fiery speech in the House, New York Federalist Barent Gardenier, a law school alumnus, denounced the embargo for impoverishing the farmers and merchants of his state. Tempers ran so high on the issue that Gardenier even fought a duel with Representative George Campbell of Tennessee over the issue.

The opposition to the embargo grew so great in parts of the North that there were threats of secession of New England states from the union. Oliver Wolcott, Jr., wrote his brother, and fellow alumnus, Frederick in December 1808:

> It must be evident to your mind, that a change of the Government, at the present time & in the present state of Parties, can only be produced by a Civil War. Who is to gain by a Civil War, not you, nor me, nor any of our Friends & Connections. . . . Let us wait; the Embargo does not distress the Federalists more than the Democrats & the former can bear it as well as the latter. When all Parties are united, as they

will be, if we are prudent, we can control the measures of the Gov't. If we once get the command, changes may be made beneficial to The Interest of the Commercial States.[1]

Following repeal of the embargo in 1809, Jefferson wrote from Monticello to his friend William Pinckney:

> I speak of that which produced a repeal of the embargo. Considerable discontent was certainly excited in Massachu-setts, but its extent was magnified infinitely beyond its reality, and an intrigue of (I believe) not more than two or three members, reputed republicans, excited in Congress a belief that we were under the alternative of civil war, or a repeal of the embargo, and the embargo was repealed.[2]

One of the Massachusetts representatives who was blamed by Jef-ferson for leading the repeal movement in Congress was alumnus Ezekiel Bacon. The other was Joseph Story, a future U.S. Supreme Court Justice, who wrote in his memoir:

> The whole influence of the Administration was directly brought to bear upon Mr. Ezekiel Bacon and myself, to seduce us from what we considered a great duty to our coun-try, and especially to New England. . . . I knew, at the time, that Mr. Jefferson had no ulterior measure in view, and was determined on protracting the embargo for an indefinite period, even for years. I was well satisfied, that such a course would not and could not be borne by New England, and would bring on a direct rebellion. It would be ruin to the

whole country. . . . Mr. Bacon and myself resisted, and measures were concerted by us, with the aid of Pennsylvania, to compel him to abandon his mad scheme. For this he never forgave me.[3]

With his popularity declining even in the South, Jefferson chose not to run for a third term in 1808, ostensibly because he was following the precedent set by George Washington. Despite the unpopularity of his administration, Jefferson's secretary of state, James Madison, easily won the nomination of the Republican Party at a caucus astutely managed by Stephen Row Bradley. The victory in the general election of Madison and his running mate, George Clinton of New York, was equally decisive.

During the first year of Madison's administration, the United States prohibited trade with both Britain and France. In 1810, the Non-Intercourse Act was directed only at Great Britain, but a young group of "war hawks" in Congress, including Henry Clay and alumnus John C. Calhoun, called for a more militant policy.

In November 1811, the House Committee on Foreign Relations, which included Calhoun and was chaired by alumnus Peter Buell Porter, published a report recommending war with Great Britain. Porter, who represented the area around Buffalo, New York, included in the report proposals for seizing parts of Canada.[4]

Under pressure from the war hawks, Madison signed a declaration of war against Great Britain on June 18, 1812. Most western and southern members of Congress supported the war, while New Englanders, who relied heavily on trade with Britain, were strongly opposed. When he was unsuccessful in counseling against war, Stephen Rowe Bradley of Vermont retired from the Senate in 1813.

The Madison war cabinet decided that a preemptive military strike into Canada, even with a relatively small and inexperienced American force, would gain a sure victory. Chosen to command the troops was General William Hull, one of Tapping Reeve's first law students, who was then also serving as governor of the newly established Michigan Territory.

He had been appointed governor in 1805 by President Jefferson, because of his broad experience during the revolution and prior success in negotiating territorial disputes with British officials and Indian tribal leaders in Canada. Hull launched an ill-fated invasion of Canada from his base in the frontier fort of Detroit on July 12, 1812. A failure by General Dearborn, commander of the American forces in the East, to communicate vital intelligence caused Hull to retreat to Detroit.

Believing Detroit was surrounded by British troops and their Indian allies, Hull surrendered the fort without firing a shot, in order to protect the resident civilians. Although captured, Hull was freed in a prisoner exchange. In 1814, at age sixty-one, he was tried by a court martial (headed by General Dearborn), which found Hull guilty of neglect of duty and cowardice. On March 8, 1814, the court issued the following sentence:

> The said Brig. Gen. Hull to be SHOT to death, two-thirds of the court concurring in the sentence. The court, in consideration of Gen. Hull's revolutionary services and his advanced age, earnestly recommend him to the mercy of the president of the United States.

After a delay of nearly two months, Madison approved the sentence but pardoned Hull, who retired from public life to his farm in

Newton, Massachusetts. A memoir written by Hull's daughter and grandson included this defense of his decisions at Detroit:

> Under these circumstances, the fall of Detroit was inevitable. If he should fight a battle and defeat the British army, this result would not be less inevitable, for a victory would not re-open his communications. Besides this, his forces were vastly inferior to those of the enemy; his provisions were nearly exhausted, and there was no possibility of obtaining a supply from any quarter. If he were to fight, he would save his own reputation, but could not save the army or territory, and he would be exposing the defenseless inhabitants of Michigan to all the horrors of Indian warfare, without a reason or an object.[5]

Over time, most of those who have studied the available evidence have concluded that Hull was overly cautious but not a coward, and that General Dearborn as well as members of Madison's war cabinet were as culpable as Hull, if not more so.[6]

At the outbreak of the war, alumnus Peter Buell Porter resigned his seat in Congress and returned to his home at Black Rock, near Buffalo, in order take an active part in the invasion of Canada. Joining the New York militia as a Brigadier General, Porter was given command of a group composed of volunteers, state militia, and Indians. He became frustrated when his commander, General Alexander Smyth, failed to invade Canada on several occasions.

When Porter called Smyth a coward in a newspaper article, Smyth challenged him to a duel, which resulted in both men missing their target and then agreeing to a truce. At the conclusion of the war, Porter received a gold medal from Congress for his military service, and President Madison offered him an appointment as Commander-in-Chief, but he declined. Both honors were in stark contrast to the fate of William Hull.

The wartime service of another alumnus, Thomas Flournoy, has also received mixed reviews that are neither as positive as Porter's nor as negative as Hull's. At the outset of the war, Flournoy left his law practice in Augusta, Georgia, to accept an appointment as a Brigadier General in the regular army.

In his first command, he replaced General James Wilkinson as head of a large military district that covered the states of Louisiana and Tennessee as well as the Mississippi Territory that included what is now the state of Alabama. On August 30, 1813, a force of about seven hundred Creek Indians destroyed Fort Mims, killing more than two hundred defenders and taking at least one hundred captives. The massacre, which spread panic among the settlers throughout the area, was blamed largely on Flournoy's lack of sufficient preparation.

Nonetheless, Flournoy wrote President Madison on October 6, 1813, to complain about the failure of his superiors to furnish him the intelligence and guidance that he needed in order to carry out his responsibilities effectively:

> Sir,
>
> The situation in which I am placed in consequence of my having received no letters from the war department in answer to some of those which I have forwarded, on subjects vitally connected with the public welfare—at war with the Creek Indians who are laying waste the frontier of this terri-

tory, at a loss how to conduct myself towards the Spaniards, who secretly abet those Indians. . . .

I am apprised, that I have no law, regulation, or order that will justify me in the course I am pursuing, but urged by necessity, & a desire to save the district I am ordered to defend, I presume to act on my own responsibility trusting to the justice of the nation, to acquit me of censure. If I err, I shall cheerfully meet an enquiry, & abide the Consequences. The Correctness of my *Motives*, cannot be questioned.[7]

One critic of America's military leadership during the war of 1812 has contended:

There was more than enough discredit to tar regulars as well as the multitudes of citizen soldiers. . . . Officers, such as Henry Dearborn, William Hull, Alexander Smyth, Thomas Flournoy, James Winchester and James Wilkinson tarnished the regular army's reputation with their ineffectiveness, misconduct, personality clashes and timidity.[8]

After the British burned the U.S. Capitol and the White House on August 24, 1814, Madison prevailed upon his secretary of state, James Monroe, to serve also as secretary of war. Six months later, the war ended with the signing of the Treaty of Ghent. Americans celebrated the end of hostilities together with the news of Andrew Jackson's victory over a larger British force in the Battle of New Orleans (even though the battle took place after the peace treaty was signed).

When James Monroe succeeded Madison as president in 1817,

one of his most pressing challenges was to fix the war department, which was in shambles by the end of the War of 1812. After three others turned down the position, John C. Calhoun agreed to become secretary of war and served through both terms of Monroe's administration (from 1817 to 1825).

Among Calhoun's greatest challenges were his dealings with General Andrew Jackson. Without authority from Washington, Jackson had captured Spanish forts, burned Seminole Indian villages and executed two British agents in Florida while successfully containing threats to settlers in Georgia and Alabama. However, Monroe was reluctant to discipline the popular hero of the Battle of New Orleans.

As war secretary, Calhoun was responsible for the management of Indian affairs, which included persuading Cherokees and other tribes to sell their lands and move far to the west. In 1817, President Monroe told a delegation of Cherokees who had moved to Arkansas:

> As long as water flows, or grass grows upon the earth, or the sun rises to show your pathway, or you kindle your camp fires, so long shall you be protected by this Government, and never again removed from your present habitations.[9]

That benign pledge contrasted sharply with the tone and content of a report Calhoun made to Congress in December 1818:

> They neither are, in fact, nor ought to be, considered as independent nations. Our views of their interest, and not their own, ought to govern them. By a proper combination of force and persuasion, of punishments and rewards, they

ought to be brought within the pales of law and civilization.
. . . Our laws and manners ought to supersede their present
savage manners and customs. Beginning with those most
advanced in civilization, and surrounded by our people, they
ought to be made to contract their settlements within reasonable bounds, with a distinct understanding that the United
States intend to make no further acquisition of land from
them, and that the settlements reserved are intended for their
permanent home. . . . Those who might not choose to submit
ought to be permitted and aided in forming new settlements
at a distance from ours. . . . It is only by causing our opinion
of their interest to prevail that they can be civilized and saved
from extinction.[10]

As Calhoun's political stature rose, he was seen as a potential
threat by the leading candidates to succeed Monroe as president—John
Quincy Adams, Henry Clay, and William Crawford. He gained influence in Washington as his relations with Jackson improved and he cul-
tivated valuable political allies. Among them were some of the
twenty-three alumni of the law school who served in Congress during
the Monroe presidency (four in the Senate and nineteen in the House).

Among his allies in the House was Micah Sterling, a contempo-
rary at Yale and the law school, who kept Calhoun informed about the
New York political scene. Others included his fellow South Carolinian,
Eldred Simkins, and John A. Cuthbert of Georgia, whom Calhoun
appointed as one of the commissioners to negotiate a treaty with the
Cherokees in 1822.[11]

Calhoun was initially a fifth candidate for president in the election of 1824. However, he failed to win the endorsement of the South

Carolina legislature, and his supporters in the key state of Pennsylvania decided to back Jackson for president under pressure from the state party leader, alumnus Henry Baldwin.

With encouragement from Pennsylvania and other states, Calhoun then decided to become a candidate for vice president and won the electoral college vote by a landslide. Finishing in second place was Senator Nathan Sanford of New York, who was then one of four alumni members of the Senate (the others being Henry Waggaman Edwards of Connecticut, Horatio Seymour of Vermont, and Nicholas Ware of Georgia).

No presidential candidate received a majority in the electoral college, and the election was ultimately resolved by the House of Representatives. Adams was declared the winner on the first ballot, even though Jackson had led Adams in both popular and electoral votes. It was widely believed at the time that Clay agreed to deliver the votes of three states to Adams in return for Adams's appointing him as secretary of state.

Referring to this "corrupt bargain," Calhoun wrote in a letter to a friend:

> Mr. Clay has made the [president] against the voice of his constituents, and has been rewarded by . . . the first office in his gift [secretary of state], the most dangerous stab, which the liberty of this country has ever received. I will not be on that side. I am with the people and shall remain so.[12]

Chapter 19
Nation's Service (1826–1836)

The scars left by the 1824 election marked the end of the so-called "era of good feelings," as Monroe's two terms in office were often called. Andrew Jackson and his congressional supporters spent the next four years effectively opposing most of the policies of President John Quincy Adams.

Adams proposed an ambitious domestic agenda that called for major federal investments in roads, canals, and other internal improvements. Champions of states' rights called such federal activism unconstitutional, while southerners grew increasingly concerned that expansion of federal activity threatened interference with the institution of slavery.

Calhoun, whose landslide victory gave him unusual independence as vice president, informed Adams in 1826 that he planned to back Jackson in the next election. He also wrote retired President Monroe in the summer of 1826:

> Never in any country . . . was there in so short a period, so complete an anarchy of political relations. Every prominent publick man feels, that he has been thrown into a new attitude, and has to reexamine his position, and reapply

principles to the situation, into which he was so unexpectedly and suddenly thrown, as if by some might[y] political revolution . . . Was he of the old Republican Party? He finds his prominent political companions, who claim and take the lead, to be the very men, against whom he had been violently arrayed till the close of the late war; and sees in the opposite rank, as enemies, those with whom he was proud to rank.[1]

In the mid-term elections of 1826, the Jacksonians gained control of both houses of Congress, but among the twenty law school alumni who were then serving in Congress (four in the Senate and sixteen in the House) the supporters of Adams outnumbered his opponents by more than two to one.

When Adams made his only cabinet change in 1828, his choice for secretary of war was alumnus Peter B. Porter, who had a distinguished service record during the War of 1812. Porter was approved by the Senate in a vote of twenty-two to eleven, with all the alumni senators voting in the affirmative. The selection of Porter by Adams was likely made at the suggestion of Henry Clay, a longtime friend of Porter's. Along with Calhoun, they had been leaders of the young "war hawks" in Congress, who pressed for war with Britain in 1812.[2]

Despite their earlier allegiance, Calhoun was on the opposite side of the political fence when Porter joined the Adams cabinet as the second alumnus to head the War Department. During the 1828 election campaign, both sides were guilty of dirty tricks. There were frequent references by the Jackson forces to the "corrupt bargain" between Adams and Clay, while Porter and Clay sought evidence of Jackson's involvement in the alleged conspiracy of Aaron Burr more than twenty years earlier.

On March 19, 1828, Clay wrote to Porter:

> I have just received information entitled to credit that
> Mrs. Blennerhasset . . . has in her possession letters from
> Andw. Jackson to her husband, incontestably proving Gen.
> Jackson's participation in Burr's conspiracy. . . .
> If she has such letters, and it should be known to some
> of the *partizans* of the Hero [Jackson], I would have no doubt
> they would get hold of them, even at the sacrifice of the life
> of the lady. . . . Let me know promptly whether you can do
> anything and what it may be.[3]

Porter and Clay abandoned their pursuit of the Burr conspiracy letters, and Jackson went on to a decisive victory in the election. A major factor in Adams's defeat was his support of a protective tariff in 1828 that became known as the "Tariff of Abominations," especially among its southern opponents.

In 1830, the debate over tariffs took a new turn when Connecticut Senator Samuel A. Foot, a law school alumnus, proposed a measure that would restrict the sale of federally owned land in the western states and territories. His aim was to help slow the westward migration of laborers out of New England manufacturing towns.

According to Jon Meacham in his prize-winning biography of Andrew Jackson,

> Foot's resolution was the occasion for what became one
> of the most significant and wide-ranging interludes in American legislative history . . . nearly half of the nation's senators
> entered the fray, delivering a total of sixty-five speeches. The

debate, [alumnus] Levi Woodbury said, "seems to have meta-morphosed the Senate, not only into a committee of the whole on the state of the Union, but into the State of the Union in all times past, present and to come."[4]

Adding to the furor, Calhoun authored a widely circulated document that laid out the doctrine of nullification and questioned the constitutionality of taxing imports without the explicit goal of raising revenue. It was his first salvo in the growing nullification crisis, which created a serious rift in his relations with Jackson. In September 1830, Calhoun wrote his friend and fellow alumnus, Virgil Maxcy, about the looming nullification crisis:

> I consider the Tariff, but as the occasion, rather than the real cause of the present unhappy state of things. The truth can no longer be disguised, that the peculiar domestick institutions of the Southern States, and the consequent direction which that and her soil and climate have given to her industry, has placed them in regard to taxation and appropriation in opposite relation to the majority of the Union; against the danger of which, if there be no protective power in the reserved rights of the states, they must in the end be forced to rebel, or submit to have . . . their domestick institutions exhausted by Colonization and other schemes, and themselves & children reduced to wretchedness. Thus situated, the denial of the right of the state to interfere constitutionally in the last resort, more alarms the thinking than all other causes.[5]

Another major legislative battle in Jackson's first term was fought over the Indian Removal Act, which authorized the government to negotiate with southern tribes for their removal to territory west of the Mississippi River and allow settlement on their lands in southern states. The Senate passed the bill by a wide margin despite strong opposition from northern senators. Among the dissenters was alumnus Peleg Sprague of Maine. Sprague attacked the plan as immoral and for its failure to provide adequate assistance to help the Cherokee and other tribes start their new lives.

The House narrowly passed the law with help from alumnus Henry W. Dwight of Massachusetts, chairman of the Committee for Indian Affairs. Following enactment of the law, Jackson appointed alumnus Henry L. Ellsworth as a commissioner to implement the resettlement. According to one account:

> This brutal policy, pursued over the next eight years, displaced some 46,000 natives. Along the forced migration that came to be called "The Trail of Tears," many died of cold, hunger and illness.[6]

On one of his trips through the West, Ellsworth was accompanied by several companions, including author Washington Irving, who wrote of his experience:

> It was early in October, 1832, that I arrived at Fort Gibson, a frontier post of the far West. . . . I had been travelling for a month past with a small party from St. Louis, up the banks of the Missouri, and along the frontier line of agencies and missions that extend from the Missouri to the Arkansas.

Our party was headed by one of the commissioners [Ellsworth] appointed by the Government of the United States to superintend the settlement of the Indian tribes migrating from the east to the west of the Mississippi. In the discharge of his duties, he was thus visiting the various out-posts of civilization. And here let me give testimony to the merits of this worthy leader of our little band. He was a native of one of the towns of Connecticut; a man in whom a course of legal practice and political life had not been able to vitiate an innate simplicity and benevolence of heart. The greater part of his days had been passed in the bosom of his family, and the society of deacons, elders, and selectmen, on the peaceful banks of the Connecticut, when suddenly he had been called to mount his steed, shoulder his rifle, and mingle among stark hunters, backwoods men, and naked savages, on the trackless wilds of the far West.[7]

Although Ellsworth's work on behalf of the Indian tribes has been largely ignored or forgotten over the years, another alumnus, George Catlin, has remained famous for the paintings he made while living among the tribes of the northern plains during the 1830s. Known as the "first artist of the West," he was, however, unsuccessful in his many attempts to sell his collection of paintings to the U.S. government.

In 1831, Jackson faced a serious political problem caused by infighting among members of his cabinet, which forced him to ask for the resignations of all but the postmaster general. Jackson chose Levi Woodbury as the new secretary of the navy. Woodbury was a former governor of New Hampshire who had been a Jackson ally in the U.S.

Senate (his later service as a U.S. Supreme Court Justice is described in Chapter Sixteen).

Having served as a member of the Senate naval committee for several years, Woodbury was aware of the challenges that were then facing the navy. High on the list was the need to protect the expanding fleet of trading and whaling vessels, which were increasing the nation's commerce around the world.

Shortly after Woodbury joined the cabinet, word arrived in Washington that several crew members of an American ship had been attacked in Sumatra while loading a cargo of spice. After conferring with Woodbury, Jackson ordered the naval frigate *Potomac* to sail for Sumatra, telling the captain to negotiate restitution first, but be willing to use force, if necessary. Deciding on arrival at his destination that negotiation would be futile, the captain sent a large landing party, which razed the town and killed more than one hundred residents.

When news of the assault reached America, Jackson's political opponents attacked him and Woodbury for the failure to attempt diplomacy at the outset. After documents were published, showing the wording of the orders given to the captain, the episode faded away.

Jackson was challenged more seriously in 1832 when South Carolina passed an ordinance declaring the 1828 and 1832 tariff acts unconstitutional and ordering that no taxes were to be collected. In response, Jackson ordered Woodbury to send several warships together with hundreds of soldiers under the command of General Winfield Scott to Charleston to enforce the laws of the land. South Carolina suspended the Nullification Ordinance, and Congress passed a law reducing the tariffs over the course of a decade. Bloodshed over the issue of states' rights was averted, but only for thirty years.

The choice of Martin Van Buren as Jackson's running mate in the

1832 election prompted Calhoun to resign the vice presidency in December 1832, after he was elected to another term in the U.S. Senate by the South Carolina legislature. He remained a Senator for much of the next twenty years and, during that period, fourteen other alumni served with him in the Senate.

By the time Jackson began his second term in 1833, he had effectively won the political battles over nullification and Indian removal but had not yet successfully completed his protracted campaign to close the second Bank of the United States. A request to renew the bank's charter was sent by the bank's management to Congress in January 1832, four years before the charter was set to expire. The legislation to recharter the bank passed both the House and Senate, but it failed to garner enough votes to overcome Jackson's veto.

Behind Jackson's opposition to the bank was a lack of trust in the "moneyed elite" who directed the bank and a belief that, as a federal institution, it had unconstitutionally encroached on states' rights to the detriment of state banks. Alumnus Henry Baldwin, who had been made a justice of the Supreme Court by Jackson, challenged his veto in one case, arguing that, "the Court cannot look to the construction given to the Constitution by the executive department as a guide."[8]

In September 1833, Jackson ordered his treasury secretary, William J. Duane, to remove the government's deposits from the national bank, but when Duane refused, Jackson replaced him with Roger Taney, who had been attorney general. The Senate failed to approve Taney's appointment but did accept Levi Woodbury as treasury secretary, and he proceeded quickly to move the deposits to what the critics called Jackson's "pet" state banks, ending the "bank war."

Woodbury was one of two members of Jackson's administration who were retained in their positions when Martin Van Buren won the

1836 presidential election. The other, Henry L. Ellsworth, was appointed by Jackson in 1836 as the founding head of the U.S. Patent Office. Although the appointment may have been meant as a reward for his service as Chief Commissioner of Indian Tribes, he was highly qualified for his new position.

Ellsworth became a champion of American inventions, including the development of Samuel Colt's revolver and Samuel Morse's telegraph. A Yale classmate of Ellsworth, Morse had received a patent after a demonstration of the telegraph in 1838, but he needed additional funds for development. Thanks to Ellsworth's successful lobbying, Congress appropriated the money for Morse to complete his work, which culminated in 1844 when the first telegraphed message was sent by Morse in Washington to his assistant in Baltimore: "What hath God wrought?"

Chapter 20
Nation's Service (1837–1861)

Martin Van Buren's first act as president in 1837 was to reappoint most of the members of Andrew Jackson's cabinet, retaining Levi Woodbury as secretary of the treasury. Thereafter, he followed his predecessor's policies so closely that some have called his presidency "Andrew Jackson's third term."

Five weeks after the inauguration, the Van Buren administration was faced with a major financial crisis that became known as the Panic of 1837. Inflation and speculative fever had become rampant after Jackson and Woodbury had ordered withdrawal of federal deposits from the national bank and transfer to state banks. The Panic, which affected almost the entire country, forced all but six banks to cease redeeming their banknotes and deposits for specie (gold or silver coins).

As treasury secretary in both administrations, Woodbury received some of the blame for the financial crisis of 1837 and its aftermath. However, he generally has received credit for his innovative reforms of the Treasury Department while acting, in effect, as the nation's first central banker. A biographical note on the website of the U.S. Treasury Department provides this objective comment:

The 1830's were a period of general prosperity, and, by 1834, the national debt had been paid off. In 1836, when the Treasury realized an unprecedented surplus, the money was turned over to the States in four installments. This extra money contributed to wild speculation and an expansion of credit resulting in a panic in 1837. Consequently, Woodbury realized the need for a system, which would enable the Government to directly administer its own funds. In 1840, Congress passed an act establishing an "independent Treasury System", where the Treasury Department, not commercial banks, was to manage the Government's funds. Much of this law was repealed the next year, but Woodbury had laid the groundwork for a more permanent independent treasury system that was eventually established in 1846.[1]

Despite Calhoun's long-standing rivalry with Van Buren, he provided important support for enactment of the Independent Treasury System when he regained his role as a leading member of the U.S. Senate. By 1840, Van Buren and Calhoun had found enough common ground for them to reconcile politically, if not personally. According to one Calhoun biographer:

All the political world was agog, and John Quincy Adams noted that evening that "the peace and alliance between Van Buren and Calhoun was manifested by the appearance of Calhoun this day at the New Year's gathering at the White House." The Whigs were, of course, distracted at the loss of a powerful ally, and all sorts of rumors flew about.[2]

Calhoun again attended the New Year's Day celebration at the White House in 1841 as a gesture of goodwill toward Van Buren, who had suffered a decisive defeat in his bid for a second term. The winning presidential candidate was William Henry Harrison, who, like Andrew Jackson, had capitalized on his fame as a military hero.

When Harrison died of pneumonia thirty-one days after his inauguration, his vice president, John Tyler, assumed the presidency with few allies in Congress or among the cabinet members appointed by Harrison. Despite his lack of partisan support, Tyler managed to achieve several important domestic and diplomatic successes, most notably, the annexation of Texas.

Much of the groundwork for annexation had been accomplished by Tyler's second secretary of state, Abel Upshur, before he was killed by the explosion of a cannon on the *U.S.S. Princeton* during a cruise for dignitaries on the Potomac River. To replace Upshur, President Tyler called on Calhoun, who successfully took over the diplomatic and political negotiations that achieved both the annexation of Texas and settlement with Great Britain of the Oregon boundary.

As pro-slavery Southerners, Calhoun and Upshur both viewed British interference with the annexation of Texas as a major threat to America's sovereign power. In the words of one recent commentator:

> Historians have understandably concentrated on the annexation of Texas as the centerpiece of Tyler's "slave-mongering diplomacy," but the foreign policy of slavery reached well beyond the Rio Grande.[3]

After completing his cabinet service at the end of Tyler's term, Calhoun wrote to a friend in May 1845:

> I was not aware until I took charge of the State Department of the immense influence, which may be exerted through it on foreign and domestic relations. . . . I had nothing to sustain me; the administration without a single advocate in Congress and . . . the acknowledged leaders of one party and both leaders and followers of the other, opposed on its leading measure, that of the Annexation; and yet with all these disadvantages, I have succeeded, by a bold unhesitating course, to secure Annexation, and leave a strong impression behind, both at home and abroad, in the short space of eleven months.[4]

Calhoun was not the only law school alumnus working to plan and promote America's foreign policy. His close friend, Virgil Maxcy, had served as the first U.S. minister to the new Kingdom of Belgium from 1837 to 1842, but died in the same accident that took the life of Abel Upshur. Other alumni who held senior diplomatic posts during the 1840s and 1850s were Charles S. Todd (minister to Russia), Nicholas Brown, III (minister to Italy), Bradley R. Wood (minister to Denmark) and John Y. Mason (minister to France).

Mason had joined Tyler's cabinet in 1844 as secretary of the Navy, filling the vacancy created when Thomas Gilmer also died in the explosion on the *Princeton*. With Calhoun as secretary of state, it marked the first time that two alumni held cabinet posts at the same time. Calhoun had served with alumni members of two earlier cabinets (Porter and Woodbury), but the vice president was not considered a cabinet member until many years later.

When James K. Polk succeeded Tyler as president in 1845, he asked Mason to join his cabinet as attorney general. They were classmates at the University of North Carolina and had maintained close political and personal ties since their days as congressional leaders during the Jackson years. Polk also rewarded another alumnus and Jackson loyalist, Levi Woodbury, by naming him to a seat on the Supreme Court. As Polk recorded in his diary: "All the members of the cabinet cordially approved the appointment."[5]

In 1846, Polk asked Mason to assume his prior role as secretary of the Navy. Mason responded that he was very satisfied with the position of attorney general, but would make the move if "it would advance the success of his administration." As it turned out, Mason's prior experience with naval operations proved valuable during the Mexican-American War, which lasted from 1846 to 1848.[6]

Following the war, Congress was faced with the thorny question of whether slavery should be allowed in the new territories. Alumnus John M. Clayton, a Whig Senator from Delaware, chaired a bipartisan committee that proposed a solution that has been called the "Clayton Compromise."

This bill, introduced in both houses of Congress, would have excluded slavery from Oregon. It also prohibited the territorial legislatures of New Mexico and California from acting on slavery and provided for appeal of slavery cases from the territorial courts to the U.S. Supreme Court. In July 1848, the bill passed easily in the Senate but was rejected by a majority in the House, which included Abraham Lincoln of Illinois and alumnus Horace Mann of Massachusetts.[7]

Polk had pledged during his election campaign that he would serve only one term, and he kept his word. When the Democrats chose

Senator Lewis Cass as their candidate for president in 1848, Martin Van Buren left the Democratic Party to head the ticket of the new Free Soil Party. The Whig Party capitalized on the turmoil in the opposition parties as well as the popularity of their candidate, Zachary Taylor, to put another military hero in the White House.

One of Taylor's early backers was alumnus Truman Smith, a Senator from Connecticut who formed a pro-Taylor group among congressional Whigs called the "Young Indians." Among its members were Abraham Lincoln and John Clayton.

In forming his cabinet, Taylor offered to make Truman Smith secretary of the newly created Home (later renamed Interior) Department, but Smith declined, preferring to retain his Senate seat. Clayton, however, left the Senate to become secretary of state. His appointment brought to twelve the number of cabinet posts held by alumni.

Taylor's choice of Clayton to head the state department was curious, as he had no prior experience with the planning or conduct of foreign policy. Indicating his apprehension in taking the job, Clayton wrote on March 16, 1849, to his friend John Crittenden, a former Senate colleague, who was then governor of Kentucky:

> In the midst of ten thousand hopes & fears, I snatch a brief moment to say that the former greatly preponderate— that I have now ten hopes to fear, and that while we are "benefitted 'round" with many cares, I firmly adhere to the belief that Taylor's administration will be one of the most glorious in our history.

Yet he warned, "If Taylor's administration fails you will find me with a drag net at the bottom of the Potomac."[8]

Clayton's most notable accomplishment was the negotiation of the Clayton-Bulwer Treaty with the British minister, Sir Henry Bulwer-Lytton, in 1850. This agreement called for joint control and operation of a canal to be built across the Isthmus of Panama. The two nations also agreed not to "exercise dominion" over any part of Central America.

Although the treaty was approved by a wide majority in the Senate, many criticized it as an erosion of the Monroe Doctrine, the U.S. policy that opposed European colonialism in the Americas. However, the treaty laid the foundation for the U.S. to build the canal by itself and on its own terms more than fifty years later. In the view of a Taylor biographer, "the Clayton-Bulwer Treaty . . . represented a giant stride in the development of the great Anglo-American relationship of the late nineteenth and twentieth centuries."[9]

Taylor died from unknown causes shortly after the Clayton-Bulwer Treaty was signed. His successor, Vice President Millard Fillmore, immediately had to deal with some highly contentious legislative proposals regarding slavery that were introduced by Senator Henry Clay.

A select Senate "Committee of Thirteen" that included alumni Daniel S. Dickinson of New York and Samuel S. Phelps of Vermont was appointed to draft legislation based on Clay's proposals. Multiple bills had been introduced as a package in an omnibus bill that failed to pass in early 1850 because of President Taylor's strong opposition.

Following Taylor's sudden death, however, the legislation was reintroduced as five separate bills that were all approved by Congress and signed into law by President Fillmore as the "Compromise of 1850." It temporarily defused sectional tensions and helped to postpone the secession crisis and the American Civil War for eleven years.

Among the principal spokesmen for the opposition in Congress was alumnus Horace Mann. An excerpt from a speech by Mann in the House on February 15, 1850, indicates how close to disunion the country had come:

> But gentlemen of the south not only argue the question of right and of honor; they go further, and they tell us what they will proceed to do if we do not yield to their demands . . . Threats of dissolution, if executed, become rebellion and treason. . . . Mr. Chairman, such collision would be war. Such forcible opposition to the government would be treason. Its agents and abettors would be traitors. Wherever this rebellion rears its crest, martial law will be proclaimed; and those found with hostile arms in their hands must prepare for the felon's doom.[10]

Among the leading supporters of Clay's proposals were Daniel Webster, known as the "Great Orator," and alumnus Daniel Dickinson, who was said to be "one of the most picturesque and popular stump speakers." Recognizing that neither of them would serve another term together in the Senate, Webster wrote Dickinson on Sept. 27, 1850:

> I hope you may live long to serve your country; but I do not think you are ever likely to see a crisis, in which you may be able to do so much, either for your own distinction or for the public good. . . . I desire to thank you and to commend your conduct out of the fullness of an honest heart. . . . I remain, my dear sir, with the truest esteem, your friend and obedient servant,
>
> Dan'l Webster.[11]

In 1853, President Franklin Pierce appointed John Y. Mason as the U.S. minister to France. A year later, Mason met with the U.S. ministers to Spain and Great Britain in Ostend, Belgium, where they drafted a secret document advocating that the U.S. purchase Cuba from Spain. It also stated that the U.S. would be "justified in wresting" the island from Spanish hands if Spain refused to sell.

Once the dispatch became public, residents of northern states were outraged at the plan to acquire Cuba, which had a large population of slaves. The Pierce administration suffered a significant setback, and the sectional conflict, rekindled by the so-called "Ostend Manifesto," brought the nation one step closer toward disunion.

Northern and southern alumni continued to play prominent public roles in the years just before and during the Civil War. In the presidential campaign of 1860, Daniel Dickinson of New York unsuccessfully sought the nomination of the Democratic Party as a compromise candidate, citing his support of southern states' rights when he was in the U.S. Senate. After the South seceded, however, Dickinson became a prominent war Democrat and supporter of President Lincoln.

A remarkably similar political reversal was made by alumnus Augustus R. Wright, who had served one term as a member of the U.S. Congress from Georgia from 1857 to 1859. As a supporter of the Union he opposed the Ordinance of Secession adopted at the Georgia Secession Convention in January 1861. Yet he accepted election to the Confederate Congress in February 1861, and was one of the architects of the Confederate Constitution.[12]

Alarmed at the growing secession of southern states, a national Peace Conference was held at Washington in early February 1861. Among the more than one hundred delegates who attended were four

Litchfield Law School alumni: Chief Justice Samuel Ames of Rhode Island, former governor Roger S. Baldwin of Connecticut, Benjamin Chew Howard from Maryland (reporter of the U.S. Supreme Court), and former Ohio Supreme Court judge John C. Wright.

The conference delegates, led by former president John Tyler of Virginia, failed in their two main objectives of stopping the tide of secession and wooing back the states that had already seceded. After the collapse of the conference, next came the battle of Fort Sumter.

Chapter 21:
End of an Era

In 1906, the last surviving alumnus of the Litchfield Law School, Henry J. Ruggles, died at the age of ninety-two. Ruggles, a New York City lawyer and Shakespearean scholar, was one of twelve students at the law school in 1832. Enrollment had peaked at fifty-five in 1813 and averaged thirty-two between 1810 and 1825, but declined steeply thereafter and averaged only ten students in its final four years, ending in 1833.

Much has been written about what caused the law school to close, but a more fundamental question is how it managed to survive as long as it did, given the many challenges it faced in its later years. Problems began as early as 1814, when Reeve reached age seventy and was required by state law to retire from the Connecticut Supreme Court.

It is likely that Reeve's supreme court duties, including a brief period as chief justice in his final year, required Gould to assume a larger share of the law school responsibilities. It also seems reasonable that at age seventy, as his biographer notes, "Judge Reeve's role in conducting the Law School began to diminish after his retirement from the bench."[1]

Whatever problems may have existed at this stage between the two partners would probably have been further complicated when Gould was appointed an associate justice of the Supreme Court in 1816. Gould's term of more than two years on the court must have required further adjustments in the partners' division of duties at the law school.

Reeve finally decided to retire from the law school in 1820 at the age of seventy-six because of his health. His wife, Betsey, wrote to a family friend, John Cotton Smith:

> Mr. Reeve . . . has been very much afflicted with a return of the spasmodic affliction in his breast which we supposed to be occasioned by a rheumatic gouty complaint which in his best health is confined to his feet which causes a slight lameness.[2]

A great deal of friction had developed between Gould and Reeve by the time of the latter's retirement, as revealed in a long letter to Reeve that year from alumnus John P. Cushman, who wrote, in part, of a conversation with Gould:

> He stated to me that the lectures by Judge Reeve were, & had for some time been thinly attended. . . . He also stated to me . . . that he had contemplated moving to New Haven to lecture . . . and that he could not consent to continue the school upon its present footing . . . longer than this fall. He expressed an opinion that the mental faculties of the Judge had in some measure failed.[3]

Some of the students favored Reeve's retirement, including William Ennis, who wrote his Brown classmate Horace Mann in 1821:

The retirement of Judge Reeve will be very beneficial to the interests of the establishment. He has become superannuated and was incapable of speaking articulately. . . . He was associated with Judge Gould for the last ten years previous to his resignation and great persuasion was requisite to induce him to surrender the whole management of his office to J. Gould.[4]

The bitterness between Reeve and Gould appears to have lasted into 1822, when Benjamin Talmadge wrote his son-in-law, John P. Cushman:

I notice your remarks respecting the Controversy between the Judges, & am truly grieved that it should be again revived. . . . Circumstanced as I am, in relation to the parties, I very early in the Controversy determined to keep myself . . .[5]

It is not known whether Reeve and Gould ever entered into a formal partnership or succession agreement during the period of more than twenty years when they ran the law school together. Gould did, however, agree to pay Reeve one-third of the net income from the law school tuition following his retirement.[6]

The total of those payments, which appear to have ended at Reeve's death in 1823, represented a very small compensation for Reeve's share of their proprietorship. There was no recognition of the substantial "goodwill" value that Reeve's name and reputation represented, as shown by the continued public references to the "Tapping Reeve Law School."[7]

During the sermon that Lyman Beecher delivered at Reeve's funeral, he mentioned that Reeve was "not affluent," and attributed his lack of wealth to "the losses he sustained in the war—the support of his aged father twenty years—the remission of charges to his poor clients—his munificence to the poor and his pious patronage of religious institutions and missionary efforts."[8]

In 1816, after leaving the Supreme Court, Reeve published his work on domestic relations, *The Law of Baron and Femme*, which is recognized as the first American legal treatise. Despite its novelty and notoriety for contending that married women had certain rights independent of their husbands, contrary to existing common law, Reeve had difficulty finding subscribers. He wrote a letter in 1819 to John P. Cushman, who was then serving in Congress, asking his assistance in persuading members of Congress, judges, and lawyers to purchase copies.[9]

Learning of Reeve's financial problems before his death, a group of alumni in Washington formed a committee in 1822 to raise funds for the benefit of their much-admired teacher. The seven principal organizers were all current or former members of the U.S. Senate and House of Representatives. Other alumni were appointed to correspond with "two or more of the judge's pupils in each state" and solicit donations. The letter mentioned that:

> In 1815 Judge Reeve lost his seat in the Superior [Supreme] Court of his state, to which he had been annually elected since the year 1798. In 1820 he was forced to discontinue his lectures. Thus deprived of his only sources of

income, he has nothing left, at the age of 78, but his dwelling house and a very small portion of land, scarcely affording his family the bare means of subsistence.[10]

There is little information as to the amount raised by the appeal and which alumni contributed, although Lyman Beecher referred to both in his funeral sermon:

> The testimonies of affectionate remembrance from his pupils . . . were cheering to the judge and especially toward the close of life, the fervency of grateful affection increased in acts of substantial munificence.[11]

The letter written by then secretary of war John C. Calhoun to U.S. Senator Horatio Seymour (one of the appeal organizers) bears out Beecher's words:

> I have added my name to the subscription attached to the resolutions, with great pleasure. For the venerable Judge I have the most sincere esteem, and will, at all times, take much pleasure in doing any act which may tend to cheer the evening of his days. Few men have passed through life more usefully, and none with a more spotless reputation. The period which I spent at Litchfield under his instruction will long be remembered by me. . . .
>
> I love to look back on it, and to dwell on all the objects connected with its remembrance. I must ask of you the favor to tender to our venerable preceptor my most sincere esteem.[12]

When Reeve retired in 1820, Gould was in the prime of life at age fifty and should have been thinking about the longer-term future of the law school. For a proprietorship structure to succeed over time requires succession planning. An essential reason for incorporating or chartering colleges and universities is to provide for their perpetual existence.

The most likely candidate to succeed Gould was probably the oldest of his seven sons, William Tracy Gould, who had finished his studies at the law school in 1818. However, William moved to Georgia in 1821 and settled in Augusta, where he practiced law before opening his own law school in 1833.

Another son, James Reeve Gould, studied at the law school in 1824 and also moved to Augusta, Georgia, in 1827 to join his brother's law firm. When James died suddenly in 1830 at the age of twenty-seven, his father was devastated. An unnamed law school student wrote in a letter to a friend at the time: "Judge Gould is so much overcome with his late family bereavement that he is unable to lecture himself. His son, however, delivers them in his stead."[13]

The reference in the letter was to a third son, George Gould, who studied at the law school in 1829 and moved in 1830 to Troy, New York, where he later became the city's mayor. Whatever the reason, the three sons who might have succeeded Gould in running the law school all passed up the opportunity and chose to move away from Litchfield.

In 1823, another problem for Gould arose when alumnus Samuel Howe co-founded a law school in Northampton, Massachusetts, that closely followed the Litchfield model. Until Howe's death in 1828, Northampton averaged ten students a year, including Franklin Pierce, a future U.S. president. Litchfield's enrollment was adversely affected by the competition from it and from another law school founded in the same period at Dedham, Massachusetts, by alumnus Theron Metcalf.

As Gould's health began to deteriorate in the late 1820s, he hired two former students to handle some of the lectures as well as the weekly examination of students. Jabez Huntington's public service commitments as a current U.S. congressman and future U.S. senator would have ruled him out as a full-time successor to Gould.

The other teaching associate, Origen Storrs Seymour, was only twenty-nine in the fall of 1833 when Gould decided to retire. However, Seymour must have abandoned Gould's plan, as it was mentioned at Gould's funeral in 1881 that after "judge Gould ceased to give instruction . . . Mr. Seymour received pupils in his office, instructing them by familiar talks and recitations, rather than by the formal method of lectures."[14]

Even if Gould had found a successor to join him sometime after Reeve retired in 1823, the law school would have required major changes in order to compete successfully with several new university-affiliated law schools, especially the ones founded at Harvard in 1817 and Yale in 1824. In the view of Yale historian John Langbein:

> The deepest flaw that would inevitably have doomed the Litchfield Law School in the long term was, I believe, its isolation, by which I mean not only its location in a remote town, but its isolation from the other intellectual currents of a university.[15]

Yet, both Harvard and Yale struggled to attract students in their early years, despite their more urban locations and university affiliations. Harvard historian Charles Warren wrote of Harvard Law School's experience:

The number of scholars, however, was small, never exceeding twenty, and finally, in 1829, becoming reduced to one. . . . Moreover, at this time, the difficulty of access to Cambridge, owing to the non-existence of rail way communication, and the rise of other law schools, more convenient for attendance, were great obstacles to the success of the Harvard Law School.[16]

The centennial history of Harvard Law School cited additional reasons for its near failure:

There were undoubtedly many reasons for this falling-off quite independent of the quality of instruction: business depression which lessened the number of law students everywhere; the multiplication of law schools in other parts of the country; the difficulty of traveling; the greater expense of education in Cambridge; the inadequate quarters of the School.[17]

It is also significant that both Harvard and Yale continued for a number of years to use the increasingly outmoded Litchfield system of teaching, based primarily on lectures and student notes. The authors of the Harvard centennial history acknowledged that:

[A]lthough these lectures were evidently modeled after those at Litchfield, they were less frequent. This inferiority in class work was little more than formal, for the Litchfield students, like those in the mediaeval universities, had to get their knowledge orally for lack of books. Having written out their own treatise, they proceeded to an individual study of it, while the students at Harvard could use the library. Yet it must be admitted that the new Law School showed no improvement in method over the old.[18]

As a rapidly growing number of legal treatises and law reports were published after 1830, students had access in the universities to a wider range of primary sources and academic analyses. Harvard and Yale eventually adopted a method that required students to read assigned texts and digests of cases in order to answer questions in class based on those assignments. This interactive process was an improvement over students passively taking notes on lectures.

A recent history of the Harvard Law School acknowledged, "In retrospect, both Harvard and Yale have envied Litchfield's success and wished to claim it as their ancestor."[19] The success and influence of the Litchfield Law School was especially well stated by Harvard Law School professor Joel Parker, who wrote in 1871:

> Probably no law school has had—perhaps I may add never will have—so great a proportion of distinguished men on its catalogue, if for no other reason, because attendance upon a Law School was then the rare exception, an advantage obtained in general only by very ambitious young men.[20]

Although the teaching method developed by Reeve and Gould eventually became outmoded, it represented a major improvement over the traditional apprenticeship model and paved the way for further innovations in legal education. In view of its influence on the course of American jurisprudence as well as the significant achievements of its distinguished alumni, the Litchfield Law School deserves greater recognition for its important role in the history of the early republic.

Notes

INTRODUCTION

1. Andrew M. Siegel, "'To Learn and Make Respectable Hereafter': The Litchfield Law School in Cultural Context," *New York University Law Review* 73 (1998): 1978.

2. The building had been moved to another location by the time it was acquired in the 1930s by a group of lawyers (including Chief Justice William Howard Taft), who restored it to its original site next to Reeve's home on South Street.

3. Student records are made available online by the Litchfield Historical Society (LHS) through *The Ledger*, which allows researchers to "browse students by name; dates of attendance; hometown, later residence; or profession." Currently, *The Ledger* contains information about 936 individuals.

4. *The Ledger* page for Robert Rankin.

5. Mark Boonshoft, "The Litchfield Network: Education, Social Capital, and the Rise and Fall of a Political Dynasty, 1784–1833," *Journal of the Early Republic* 34, no. 4 (Winter 2014): 563.

6. The total includes Charles Herman Ruggles, who was chief judge of the New York Court of Appeals, and Nathan Sanford, who was Chancellor of New York when that was the highest judicial office in the state. It also includes Oliver Spencer Halstead and Kensey Johns, Jr., who were Chancellors of New Jersey and Delaware, respectively.

CHAPTER 1: REVOLUTIONARY LITCHFIELD

1. George Catlin Woodruff, *History of the Town of Litchfield, Connecticut* (Litchfield, CT: C. Adams, 1845), p. 45.

2. Ron Chernow, *Alexander Hamilton* (New York: Penguin, 2005), p. 43.

3. James McLachlan, *Princetonians, 1748–1768: A Biographical Dictionary* (Princeton, NJ: Princeton University Press, 2015), p. 440; Mark Boonshoft, "The Great Awakening," in *The American Revolution Reborn*, ed. Patrick Spero and Michael Zuckerman (Philadelphia: University of Pennsylvania Press, 2016), p. 180.

4. Gerard W. Gawalt, "Massachusetts Legal Education in Transition, 1766–1840," *The American Journal of Legal History* 17, no. 1 (January 1973), pp. 27–50.

5. Thomas Jefferson and Henry Augustine Washington, *The Life and Letters of Thomas Jefferson: Being His Autobiography and Select Correspondence* (New York: Edwards, Pratt and Foster, 1858), p. 3.

6. Albert W. Alschuler, "Rediscovering Blackstone," *University of Pennsylvania Law Review* 145, no. 1 (November 1996).

7. Sir William Blackstone, *Commentaries on the Laws of England*, Vol. 1 (London: Clarendon Press, 1768), p. 31.

8. Rachel Carley, *Litchfield: The Making of a New England Town* (Litchfield, CT: Litchfield Historical Society), p. 87.

9. Ibid.

10. Aaron Burr and Matthew Livingston Davis, *Memoirs of Aaron Burr: With Miscellaneous Selections from His Correspondence*, Vol. 1 (New York: Harper and Brothers, 1837), p. 46.

11. Ibid., pp. 53–55.

12. Franklin Bowditch Dexter, *Biographical Sketches of the Graduates of Yale College: With Annals of the College History*, Vol. 6, *May 1763–July 1778* (New York: Holt, 1903), pp. 444–448.

13. Stephen R. Bradley, *Letters of a Revolutionary War Patriot and Vermont Senator,* ed. Dore Bradley Carpenter (Jefferson, NC: McFarland & Co, 2008), p. 23.

14. *Memoirs of Aaron Burr,* p. 75.

15. Research for this book uncovered seven previously unknown law school alumni (including William Hull), and, hopefully, it will encourage others to discover additional alumni to add to the school records.

CHAPTER 2: PIONEERING LAW SCHOOL

1. Timothy Dwight, *Travels in New-England and New-York,* Vol. IV (London: William Baynes and Son, 1823), p. 295.

2. Charles Warren, *History of the Harvard Law School and of Early Legal Conditions in America,* Vol. 1 (New York: Lewis Publishing, 1908), p. 182.

3. See Marian C. McKenna, *Tapping Reeve and The Litchfield Law School* (New York: Oceana Publications, 1986) p. 139, who states that "Litchfield's tuition was never raised."

4. Burton S. Hill, "Litchfield, First American Law School," *Quarterly Review: A Journal of University Perspectives* 56 (1949): p. 225.

5. Hill, Appendix B.

6. Andrew M. Siegel, "'To Learn and Make Respectable Hereafter': The Litchfield Law School in Cultural Context," *New York University Law Review* 73 (1998): 1978.

7. Samuel Church, "Address," in "Litchfield County Centennial Celebration" (Hartford, CT: Edwin Hunt, 1851), p. 48.

8. Arthur Zilversmit, "Quok Walker, Mumbet, and the Abolition of Slavery in Massachusetts," *The William and Mary Quarterly* 25, no. 4 (October 1968), p. 622–624.

9. David S. Boardman, "Sketches of the Early Lights of the Litchfield Bar" (Litchfield, CT: James Humphrey, Jr., 1860), p. 6.

10. Ibid., p. 7.

11. In 1806, the number of superior court judges was increased from five to nine and those judges, sitting together, constituted the supreme court.

12. Simeon Baldwin, "James Gould, 1770–1838," in *Great American Lawyers,* Vol. 2, ed. William Draper Lewis (Philadelphia: John C. Winston Company, 1907), p. 456.

13. Quoted in Warren, "Harvard Law School," p. 183.

14. Tapping Reeve to Abraham Kirby, April 29, 1780, Ephraim Kirby Papers, Duke University.

15. John C. Calhoun to Tapping Reeve, February 10, 1810, Litchfield Historical Society.

16. John Cotton Smith to Tapping Reeve, December 2, 1817, Litchfield Historical Society.

CHAPTER 3: A NATIONAL PERSPECTIVE

1. John H. Langbein, "Chancellor Kent and the History of Legal Literature," Faculty Scholarship Series, paper 549 (1993), digitalcommons.law.yale.edu/fss_papers/549.

2. *The Ledger.*

3. William Montgomery Meigs, *The Life of John Caldwell Calhoun,* Vol. 1 (New York: Neale Publishing Company, 1917), p. 74.

4. William Cumming to Thomas Cumming, July 7, 1806 (Duke University).

5. Roger S. Baldwin to Simeon Baldwin, *Baldwin Family Papers, 1734–1977* (New Haven: New Haven Museum).

6. John Young Mason to Edmunds Mason, January 28, 1818 (Virginia Historical Society).

7. Fred B. Devitt, Jr., "One Hundred Eightieth Anniversary Feature: William and Mary: America's First Law School," *William & Mary Law Review* 2, issue 2 (1960).

8. Mark Boonshoft, "The Litchfield Network: Education, Social Capital, and the Rise and Fall of a Political Dynasty, 1784–1833," *Journal of the Early Republic* 34, no. 4 (Winter 2014): 568.

9. Paul D. Carrington, "The Revolutionary Idea of University Legal Education," *William & Mary Law Review* 31 (1990), pp. 549, 552.

10. Alfred Zantzinger Reed, "Training for the Public Profession of the Law" (New York City, 1921), p. 128–129.

11. Charles William Darling, *Memorial to my Honored Kindred* (Utica, NY, 1888), p. 54.

12. Andrew M Siegel, "'To Learn and Make Respectable Hereafter': The Litchfield Law School in Cultural Context," *New York University Law Review* 73 (1998): 2022.

CHAPTER 4: TEACHING LAW AS SCIENCE

1. Dwight C. Kilbourn, *The Bench and Bar of Litchfield County, Connecticut, 1709–1909*, Privately published (1909), p. 187.

2. Roger Sherman Baldwin to Simeon Baldwin, December 7, 1812, Yale University.

3. Simeon E. Baldwin, "James Gould, 1770–1838," in *Great American Lawyers*, Vol. 2, ed. William Draper Lewis (Philadelphia: John C. Winston Company, 1907), pp. 461, 463.

4. Edward Deering Mansfield, *Personal Memories, Social, Political, and Literary: With Sketches of Many Noted People, 1803–1843* (Cincinnati: Robert Clarke & Co., 1879), pp. 127–128.

5. Stephen M. Sheppard, "Casebooks, Commentaries, and Curmudgeons: An Introductory History of Law in the Lecture Hall," *Iowa Law Review* 82 (1997), p. 566; McKenna, *Tapping Reeve and The Litchfield Law School* (Oceana Publications, 1986), pp. 166–167.

6. The nine students and their time at the law school are Eliphalet Dyer (1790–1793); Asa Bacon Jr. (1794); Seth P. Staples (1798); Daniel Sheldon Jr. (1798); Aaron Burr Reeve (1802–1807); Ely Warner (1808–1809); Timothy Follett

(1812–1813); Origen Storrs Seymour ((1824–1825) and George Flagg Mann (1826–1827); see, Charles C. Goetsch, "The Litchfield Law School: A Modern View," copy of paper at Litchfield Historical Society.

7. Whitney S. Bagnall, "Composite Curriculum at Litchfield Law School based on lectures of Tapping Reeve, 1790–1798" and "Composite Curriculum of Litchfield Law School, 1812–1813" at documents.law.yale.edu. (2013). The notes are at the Litchfield Historical Society, the Connecticut Historical Society, the Connecticut State Library, Yale Law Library, the John Hay Library of Brown University, and the New York State Library.

8. See https://documents.law.yale.edu/litchfield-law-school-sources and https://documents.law.yale.edu/digitized-authors for a list of all known digitized Litchfield Law School sources.

9. John H. Langbein, "Blackstone, Litchfield, and Yale: The Founding of the Yale Law School," in *History of the Yale Law School*, ed. Anthony T. Kronman (New Haven, CT: Yale University Press, 2004), p. 29.

10. Lawrence M. Friedman, *A History of American Law*, 3rd ed. (New York: Simon and Schuster, 2005), p. 239.

11. James Gould, "Law School at Litchfield," *United States Law Journal and Civilian's Magazine* (1823), p. 404.

12. Thomas Telfair to Alexander Telfair, April 2, 1807, Duke University.

13. Augustus C. Hand to Samuel Hand, November 12, 1827.

14. Langbein, "Blackstone, Litchfield, and Yale," p. 33.

15. Karen Beck, "One Step at a Time: The Research Value of Law Student Notebooks," *Law Library Journal* 91, 1 (Winter 1999), p. 42; Angela Fernandez, "Copying and Copyright Issues at the Litchfield Law School," University of Toronto Legal Research Studies Series 08-13, https://papers.ssrn.com/sol3/papers.cfm?abstract_id=1160023, p. 8.

16. Simeon E. Baldwin, "The United States Law Journal of 1822" (1918), Faculty Scholarship Series, paper 4309, pp. 45–46.

17. Angela Fernandez and Markus D. Dubber, eds., *Law Books in Action: Essays on the Anglo-American Legal Treatise* (Portland, OR: Hart Publishing, 2012).

18. Tapping Reeve, *The Law of Baron and Femme, of Parent and Child, Guardian and Ward, Master and Servant*, 3rd ed. (Albany, NY: W. Gould, 1862), p. 220.

19. Kilbourn, p. 187.

20. Reeve, p. vii.

21. Kilbourn, pp. 24, 26.

22. Oliver Wendell Holmes, Jr., *The Common Law* (Boston: Little, Brown, 1909), p. 1.

CHAPTER 5: STUDENT MOOT COURTS

1. Litchfield Law School, *The Litchfield Law School, 1784–1833* (Litchfield, CT: Press of the Litchfield Enquirer, 1900), p. 5.

2. Charles Warren, *History of the Harvard Law School and of Early Legal Conditions in America*, Vol. 1 (New York: Lewis Publishing Company, 1908), p. 334.

3. Augustus Hand to Samuel Hand, January 30, 1829, LHS.

4. For a list of the "privileged books," see Marian C. McKenna, *Tapping Reeve and The Litchfield Law School* (Oceana Publications, 1986), p. 116.

5. William C. Cumming to Thomas Cumming, December 28, 1806, Litchfield Historical Society.

6. Copy of advertisement held at Litchfield Historical Society.

7. Doron S. Ben-Atar and Richard D. Brown, *Taming Lust* (Philadelphia: University of Pennsylvania Press, 2014), p. 60.

8. Payne Kenyon Kilbourne, "Sketches and Chronicles of the Town of Litchfield, Connecticut" (Hartford, CT: Press of Case, Lockwood and Company, 1859), p. 148.

9. Charles Warren, *A History of the American Bar* (Boston: Little, Brown, 1911), p. 184.

10. Paul DeForest Hicks, *Joseph Henry Lumpkin: Georgia's First Chief Justice* (Athens: University of Georgia Press, 2002), p. 11.

11. Donald F. Melhorn, Jr., "A Moot Court Exercise: Debating Judicial Review Prior to *Marbury v. Madison*," *Constitutional Commentary* 12 (Winter 1995): 327–354.

12. Melhorn, *Lest We be Marshall'd* (Akron, OH: University of Akron Press, 2003), pp. 53–54.

13. Melhorn, "A Moot Court Exercise," p. 349.

14. Ibid., p. 351.

15. Ibid.

16. Ibid., p. 352.

CHAPTER 6: AMERICANIZING THE COMMON LAW

1. Ellen Holmes Pearson, *Remaking Custom: Law and Identity in the Early American Republic* (Charlottesville: University of Virginia Press, 2011), p. 25.

2. Ephraim Kirby, *Reports of cases adjudged in the Superior Court of Connecticut; with some determinations in the Supreme Court of Errors* (Litchfield, CT: Collier & Adam, 1789).

3. Alan V. Briceland, "Ephraim Kirby: Pioneer of American Law Reporting, 1789," *The American Journal of Legal History* 16, no. 4 (October 1972), pp. 311–312.

4. Ibid., p. 315.

5. http://founders.archives.gov/documents/Jefferson/01-35-02-0485.

6. Jesse Root, *Reports of Cases Adjudged in the Superior Court and Supreme Court of Errors, From July 1789 to June 1798*, Vol. 2 (Hartford, CT: Hudson and Goodwin, 1802).

7. E. Thompson Company, "The Litchfield Law School," *Law Notes* 4 (1900), p. 208.

8. James C. Mohr, *Abortion in America: The Origins and Evolution of National Policy* (New York: Oxford University Press, 1979), pp. 22–3.

9. Richard A. Danner, "More than Decisions: Reviews of American Law Reports in the Pre-West Era," Duke Law School Public Law & Legal Theory Series, No. 2015–27 (June 19, 2015), p. 16.

10. Briceland, p. 317.

11. *The American Jurist and Law Magazine*, Volume 24 (1841), p. 248.

12. Danner, p. 18.

13. Paine helped Wheaton to prepare the United States Supreme Court Reports between 1816 and 1827. Separately, Paine was the reporter for *Paine's United States Circuit Court Reports*, and in 1830 was the joint author with John Duer of *Paine and Duer's Practice in Civil Actions and Proceedings at Law in the State of New York*.

14. Wheaton v. Peters, 33 US (8 Pet.) 591 (1834). Law School alumnus Justice Henry Baldwin dissented. The Supreme Court did recognize federal common law in later cases.

15. Craig Joyce, "A Curious Chapter in the History of Judicature: *Wheaton v. Peters* and the Rest of the Story (of Copyright in the New Republic)," *Houston Law Review* 42 (2005), p. 325.

CHAPTER 7: STUDENT LIFE IN LITCHFIELD

1. Emily Noyes Vanderpoel, *Chronicles of a Pioneer School from 1792 to 1833: Being the History of Miss Sarah Pierce and her Litchfield School* (Cambridge, MA: Harvard University Press, 1903), p. 28.

2. William Ennis to Horace Mann, March 4, 1821, Massachusetts Historical Society.

3. Edward Deering Mansfield, *Personal Memories, Social, Political, and Literary* (Cincinnati: Robert Clarke & Co., 1879), p. 122.

4. Mansfield, p. 124. Benjamin Tallmadge is best known for his service during the Revolutionary War as an officer in the Continental Army, especially as leader of the Culper Ring, a network of spies in British-occupied New York. Following the war, Tallmadge settled in Litchfield and was elected to the U.S. House of Representatives.

5. Vanderpoel, p. 297.

6. James Averell, Jr., to William Holt Averell, September 26, 1817, New York State Historical Association Library.

7. Lyman Beecher, *Autobiography, Correspondence, &c. of Lyman Beecher*, Vol. 1, ed. Charles Beecher (New York: Harper & Brothers, 1864), p. 209.

8. Ibid., p. 224.

9. Quoted in George C. Boswell, ed., *Litchfield Book of Days* (Litchfield, CT: 1899), pp. 116–117.

10. Boswell, p. 117.

11. Mansfield, *Personal Memories*, p. 129.

12. Cyrus Alden to Thomas Alden, September 25, 1808, Litchfield Historical Society.

13. John Young Mason to his father, January 28, 1818, Virginia Historical Society.

14. Rachel Carley, *Litchfield: The Making of a New England Town* (Litchfield, CT: Litchfield Historical Society, 2011), p. 94.

15. Mark Boonshoft, "The Litchfield Network: Education, Social Capital, and the Rise and Fall of a Political Dynasty, 1784–1833," *Journal of the Early*

Republic 34, no. 4 (Winter 2014), p. 563.

16. Andrew M. Siegel, "'To Learn and Make Respectable Hereafter': The Litchfield Law School in Cultural Context," *New York University Law Review* 73 (1998): 1981.

17. William Greene to Abigail Lyman, December 29, 1818, Cincinnati Historical Society.

18. Vanderpoel, p. 334.

19. Ibid., p. 128.

20. Ibid.

CHAPTER 8: FADING FEDERALISTS

1. The Democratic-Republican Party, formed by Jefferson and Madison in opposition to the Federalist Party, is often referred to as the Republican Party, but to avoid confusion with the later Republican Party (headed by Lincoln), it is called the Jeffersonian Party in this book.

2. Joseph Howard Parks, *The House of Blue Light* (Baton Rouge: Louisiana State University Press, 1992), p. 2.

3. Ephraim Kirby to Aaron Burr, June 4, 1801, forwarded by Burr to Thomas Jefferson. http://founders.archives.gov/documents/Jefferson/01-34-02-0206.

4. William C. Cumming to his father, December 28, 1806, Litchfield Historical Society.

5. Cyrus Alden to Kilbourne Whitman, October 30, 1808, Massachusetts Historical Society.

6. Andrew M. Siegel, "'To Learn and Make Respectable Hereafter': The Litchfield Law School in Cultural Context," *New York University Law Review* 73 (1998): 2012.

7. Robert J. Imholt, "Timothy Dwight, Federalist Pope of Connecticut," *The New England Quarterly* 73, no. 3 (September 2000): 402–40. Dwight and

Reeve had personal ties as Sally Reeve and Dwight were grandchildren of Jonathan Edwards, the architect of a revivalist movement known as the First Great Awakening.

8. Margaret L. Coit, *John C. Calhoun: American Portrait* (Boston: Houghton Mifflin, 1950), p. 157.

9. Samuel H. Fisher, "Why Two Connecticut Yankees Went South," *The Florida Historical Quarterly* 18, no. 1 (July 1939): 36.

10. John Quincy Adams, *Documents Relating to New-England Federalism*, ed. Henry Adams (Boston: Little, Brown, 1905), p. 338.

11. Ibid., pp. 342–343.

12. Letter from John C. Calhoun to Mrs. Floride Calhoun, December 1805.

13. Tapping Reeve, "The Sixth of August or The Litchfield Festival Address" (Hartford, CT: Hudson and Goodwin, 1806), p. 5.

14. Phillip Blumberg, *Repressive Jurisprudence in the Early American Republic: The First Amendment and the Legacy of English Law* (Cambridge: University of Cambridge Press, 2010), p. 158.

15. Thomas Jefferson to James Madison, September 18, 1807, *Republic of Letters* note 32, 1497–1498.

16. J. R. Scafidel, "A Georgian in Connecticut: A. B. Longstreet's Legal Education," *The Georgia Historical Quarterly* 61, no. 3 (Fall 1977): 224.

17. Thomas J. DiLorenzo, "Yankee Confederates: New England Secession Movements Prior to the War Between the States," in David Gordon, ed., *Secession, State and Liberty* (New Brunswick, NJ: Transaction Publishers, 1998).

18. John Young Mason to his father, January 28, 1818, Virginia Historical Society.

19. Boonshoft, *The Litchfield Network*, p. 585.

CHAPTER 9: SLAVERY

1. Ellen Holmes Pearson, *Remaking Custom: Law and Identity in the Early American Republic* (Charlottesville: University of Virginia Press, 2011), pp. 119–121.

2. Ibid., p. 120.

3. Slavery and Abolition Manuscript, Judge Tapping Reeve, et al., sold by Swann Auction Galleries. February 21, 2008.

4. Tapping Reeve, *The Law of Baron and Femme, of Parent and Child, Guardian and Ward, Master and Servant*, 3rd ed. (Albany, NY: W. Gould, 1862), p. 484.

5. https://userpages.umbc.edu/~bouton/History407/SlaveStats.htm.

6. Marian C. McKenna, *Tapping Reeve and The Litchfield Law School* (Oceana Publications, 1986), p. 52.

7. William L. Andrews and Regina E. Mason, eds., *Life of William Grimes, the Runaway Slave* (New York: Oxford University Press, 2008), pp. 58, 66–67.

8. Ibid., p. 101.

9. Laura Copland, "The Rise and Fall of Moses Simons: A Black Lawyer in the New York City Criminal Court, 1816–1820," *African Americans in New York Life and History* 37 (2013): 81–114.

10. Donald E. Williams, Jr., *Prudence Crandall's Legacy: The Fight for Equality in the 1830s, Dred Scott, and Brown v. Board of Education* (Middletown, CT: Wesleyan University Press, 2014), p. 261.

CHAPTER 10: WESTWARD HO!

1. Princeton University Library, Rare Books and Manuscripts Collections.

2. Joseph Green Butler, *History of Youngstown and the Mahoning Valley, Ohio*, Vol. 1 (Chicago: American Historical Society, 1921), pp. 111, 409.

3. Ibid., p. 249.

4. Donald F. Melhorn, Jr., *Lest We Be Marshall'd* (Akron, OH: University of Akron Press, 2008), ch. 5.

5. George B. Kulp, *Families of the Wyoming Valley: Biographical, Genealogical and Historical. Sketches of the bench and bar of Luzerne County, Pennsylvania* (Wilkes-Barre, PA: E. B. Yordy, 1885), p. 1051.

6. George Catlin, *Manners, Customs, and Conditions of the North American Indians* (Courier Corporation, 1973), p. viii.

7. John McAuley Palmer, ed., *The Bench and Bar of Illinois: Historical and Reminiscent*, Vol. 1 (Chicago: The Lewis Publishing Co., 1899), pp. 180–181.

8. Roger Billings, *Abraham Lincoln, Esq.: The Legal Career of America's Greatest President*, (Lexington: University Press of Kentucky, 2010), pp. 93–96.

9. Charles Lanman, *The Life of William Woodbridge* (Washington: Blanchard & Mohun, 1867), p. 133.

10. http://www.encyclopediaofarkansas.net.

11. https://www.roselawfirm.com/history/; Hillary Rodham Clinton is a former partner in the Rose Law Firm.

12. Daniel J. Boorstin, *The Mysterious Science of the Law: An Essay on Blackstone's Commentaries* (Chicago: University of Chicago Press, 1941), p. 4.

CHAPTER 11: THE DEEP SOUTH

1. Perry G. Miller, *The Life of the Mind in America: From the Revolution to the Civil War* (New York: Harcourt, 1965), p. 109.

2. Charles Warren, *A History of the American Bar* (Boston: Little, Brown, 1911), p. 322.

3. *The Ledger* allows researchers to "Browse students by name; dates of attendance; hometown, later residence; or profession." At the time of my research,

results for·"hometown" showed 306 students from Connecticut and 201 by "later residence."

4. Thomas Rogers Hunter, "Litchfield on the Savannah: William Tracy Gould and the Deep South's First Law School," *The Journal of Southern Legal History* 19 (2011): 181.

5. Mark Boonshoft, "The Litchfield Network: Education, Social Capital, and the Rise and Fall of a Political Dynasty, 1784–1833," *Journal of the Early Republic* 34, no. 4 (Winter 2014): 586–587.

6. Hunter, p. 181. See also Lawrence B. Custer, "The Litchfield Law School: Educating Southern Lawyers in Connecticut," *Georgia Journal of Southern Legal History* 2 (1993): 194 and footnote 55.

7. William J. Northen, ed., *Men of Mark in Georgia*, Vol. 3 (Atlanta: A. B. Caldwell, 1910), p. 244.

8. Walter B. Hill, "The Supreme Court of Georgia," *The Green Bag* 4 (Boston Book Company, 1892), p. 21.

9. Michael O'Brien, ed., *All Clever Men, Who Make Their Way: Critical Discourse in the Old South* (Athens: University of Georgia Press, 2008), p. 376.

10. Hunter, p. 184.

11. Ibid., p. 194.

12. Ibid., pp. 198–199.

13. Ibid., pp. 222–223.

14. Daniel R. Coquillette and Bruce A. Kimball, *On the Battlefield of Merit: Harvard Law School, the First Century* (Cambridge, MA: Harvard University Press, 2015), p. 228.

15. J. R. Scafidel, "A Georgian in Connecticut: A. B. Longstreet's Legal Education," *The Georgia Historical Quarterly* 61, no. 3 (Fall 1977): 222–232.
16. Joseph B. Cumming, "The Cumming-McDuffie Duels," *The Georgia Historical Quarterly* 44, no. 1 (March 1960): 18–40.

17. Lyman Beecher, *The Remedy for Duelling: A Sermon, Delivered Before the Presbytery of Long-Island, at the Opening of Their Session, at Aquebogue, April 16, 1806* (New York: J. Seymour, printer, 1809).

CHAPTER 12: NEW YORK CITY

1. Although definitions of the "Mid-Atlantic" region differ, it refers here to the states of Delaware, Maryland, New Jersey, Pennsylvania, and New York, as well as the District of Columbia. See Frederick Jackson Turner, *The Frontier in American History* (New York: Henry Holt, 1921), pp. 27–28.

2. Robert Taylor Swaine, *The Cravath Firm and Its Predecessors, 1819–1947*, Vol. 1 (The Lawbook Exchange, 2007), p. 6.

3. Donald J. Paisley, "Lewis Bartholomew Woodruff," in *The Judges of the New York Court of Appeals: A Biographical History*, ed. Hon. Albert M. Rosenblatt (New York: Fordham University Press, 2007); *King v. Talbot* (40 NY 85, 86).

4. Proceedings on the Death of Lewis B. Woodruff, September 15, 1875 (New York Bar Association, 1875).

5. Axel Madsen, *John Jacob Astor: America's First Multimillionaire* (New York: John Wiley & Sons, 2002), p. 246.

6. Francis Schell, *Memoir of the Hon. Augustus Schell*, Privately printed (1885), appendix, pp. 48–49.

7. Walter Barrett, *The Old Merchants of New York City* (New York: Carleton, 1870), p. 93.

8. *The American Annual Cyclopædia and Register of Important Events of the Year 1870* (New York: D. Appleton, 1871), p. 214.

CHAPTER 13: UPSTATE NEW YORK

1. Lois Kimball Mathews, *The Expansion of New England: The Spread of New England Settlement and Institutions to the Mississippi River, 1620–1865* (Boston and New York: Houghton Mifflin, 1909), p. 149–150.

2. George Baker Anderson, *Landmarks of Rensselaer County* (Syracuse, NY: D. Mason and Company, 1897), p. 227.

3. Tapping Reeve, *The Law of Baron and Femme, of Parent and Child, Guardian and Ward, Master and Servant*, 3rd ed. (1862), p. 327.

4. Reports of Cases Argued and Determined in the Supreme Court, 2nd ed., Pawling v. Wilson, 13 Johns (1816).

5. Edmund Quincy, *Life of Josiah Quincy of Massachusetts* (Boston: Ticknor and Fields, 1868), p. 134.

6. Samuel Miles Hopkins and Sarah Hopkins Bradford, *Sketch of the Public and Private Life of Samuel Miles Hopkins, of Salem, Connecticut* (Rochester, NY: The Society, 1898) p. 17.

7. Ibid., p. 51.

8. William Farley Peck, *History of Rochester and Monroe County, New York: From the Earliest Historic Times to the Beginning of 1907*, Vol. 1 (New York: Pioneer Publishing Company 1908), p. 63.

9. William Preston Vaughn, *The Anti-Masonic Party in the United States: 1826–1843* (Lexington: University Press of Kentucky, 2015), p. ix.

10. The Lehrman Institute, "Daniel S. Dickinson (1806–1884)," in *Mr. Lincoln and New York* (New York: The Lehrman Institute, 2002–2019). http://www.mrlincolnandnewyork.org/new-yorkers/daniel-s-dickinson-1806-1884/.

11. Gerald Gunther, *Learned Hand: The Man and the Judge* (New York: Oxford University Press, 2010), p. 11.

CHAPTER 14: NEW ENGLAND

1. Benjamin Homer Hall, *History of Eastern Vermont: From Its Earliest Settlement to the Close of the Eighteenth Century* (New York: D. Appleton & Co, 1858), pp. 596–598.

2. Walter H. Crockett, *Vermont: The Green Mountain State*, Vol. 1 (New York: The Century History Company, 1921), p. 437.

3. Jacob G. Ullery, *Men of Vermont: An Illustrated Biographical History of Vermonters and Sons of Vermont* (Brattleboro, VT: Transcript Publishing, 1894), p. 116.

4. Benjamin Franklin Tefft, *Life of Daniel Webster* (Philadelphia: Porter and Coates, 1854), p. 189.

5. Richard Henry Dana, Jr., "A Tribute to Judge Sprague," Privately printed (Boston, Alfred Mudge & Son, 1864), pp. 14–15. The jurisdiction of federal district and circuit court judges has changed substantially over the years.

6. David A. Moss, *Democracy* (Cambridge, MA: Harvard University Press, 2017), p. 220.

7. Charles Henry Ambler, ed., "Correspondence of Robert M. T. Hunter, 1826–1876" (U.S. Government Printing Office, 1918), p. 80.

8. Erik J. Chaput and Russell DeSimone, "The Road Not Taken: John Brown Francis and the Dorr Rebellion," Providence College, Digital Commons (2014), PDF (text searchable), pp. 1–10. https://digitalcommons.providence.edu/dorr_scholarship/2/.

9. Wesley W. Horton, *The Connecticut State Constitution* (New York: Oxford University Press, 2012), p. 11.

10. Richard Joseph Purcell, *Connecticut in Transition, 1775–1818* (American Historical Association, 1918), p. 376.

11. Letter from Pierpont Edwards to Thomas Jefferson, *The Papers of Thomas Jefferson*, Vol. 37 (4 March to 30 June 1802), p. 210.

12. *The Congregational Quarterly*, Volume 5 (Boston: Edward L. Balch, 1863), pp. 5–6.

CHAPTER 15: BUSINESS AND COMMERCE

1. Phillip Thomas Tucker, *America's Forgotten First War for Slavery and Genesis of the Alamo*, Vol. 1 (Portland, OR: PublishNation LLC, 2017), pp. 178–180.

2. Margaret Swett Henson, "Trinity Land Company," in Handbook of Texas Online, accessed February 18, 2018, http://www.tshaonline.org/handbook/online/articles/uft01.

3. Donald L. Miller and Louis P. Masur, *The Rise of Capitalism: The Unseen Hand* (2000) WGBH Educational Foundation, p. 3. https://www.learner.org/series/biographyofamerica/prog07/transcript/index.html.

4. Freeman Hunt, William B. Dana, Isaac Smith Homans, *Merchants' Magazine and Commercial Review*, Vol. 31 (1854), p. 207.

5. Robert B. Shaw, "The Great Schuyler Stock Fraud," *Railroad History* no. 141 (Autumn 1979): 5–18.

6. James Grant Wilson and John Fiske, eds., *Appleton's Cyclopaedia of American Biography*, Vol 3 (New York: D. Appleton and Company, 1887), p. 544.

7. Edwin G. Burrows and Mike Wallace, *Gotham: A History of New York City to 1898* (New York: Oxford University Press, 1998), pp. 445, 615.

8. Chemical Bank and Trust Company, *History of the Chemical Bank: 1823–1913*, Privately printed (1913), p. 88.

CHAPTER 16: SUPREME COURT JUSTICES

1. The terms "alumnus/alumni" are used rather than "graduate/graduates" because Litchfield Law School was not affiliated with a university and did not award degrees. Justice Ruth Bader Ginsburg started her law studies at Harvard but received her law degree from Columbia.

2. Another Litchfield alumnus, Levi Woodbury, has been erroneously credited with the distinction of being the first Supreme Court Justice to attend law school, but Woodbury did not join the court until 1846, sixteen years after Baldwin.

3. Charles Warren, *The Supreme Court in United States History*, vol. 2 (Boston: Little, Brown, 1922), p. 242.

4. Mark Levin, *Men in Black: How the Supreme Court Is Destroying America* (New York: Simon and Schuster, 2006), pp. 2–3.

5. Paul Finkelman, ed., *The Supreme Court: Controversies, Cases, and Characters from John Jay to John Roberts*, vol. 1 (Santa Barbara, CA: ABC-CLIO, 2014), p. 238.

6. Timothy S. Huebner, *The Taney Court: Justices, Rulings, and Legacy* (Santa Barbara, CA: ABC-CLIO, 2003), p. 84.

7. Donald B. Cole, *Martin van Buren and the American Political System* (Princeton, NJ: Princeton University Press, 2014), p. 388.

8. Huebner, p. 87.

9. Martin Naparsteck, *The Trial of Susan B. Anthony: An Illegal Vote, a Courtroom Conviction and a Step Toward Women's Suffrage* (Jefferson, NC: McFarland, 2014), p. 143.

10. *New York Times* (December 9, 1872), p. 4.

CHAPTER 17: NATION'S SERVICE (1789–1807)

1. One hundred one alumni were elected U.S. representatives, but John Starke Edwards died before assuming his seat.

2. The vice president is not officially a member of the cabinet.

3. Paul D. Carrington, "The Theme of Early American Law Teaching: The Political Ethics of Francis Lieber," *Journal of Legal Education* 42 (1992): 346.

4. Steve Sheppard, ed., *The History of Legal Education in the United States: Commentaries and Primary Sources*, Vol. 1 (Pasadena, CA: Salem Press, Inc., 1999), p. 13.

5. James E. Cronin, ed., *The Diary of Elihu Hubbard Smith (1771–1798)* (Philadelphia: American Philosophical Society, 1973), p. 28.

6. Ron Chernow, *Alexander Hamilton* (New York: Penguin, 2005), p. 620.

7. Kathryn Turner, "The Midnight Judges," *University of Pennsylvania Law Review* 109 (1961): 506.

8. Ibid., p. 507.

9. James Parton, *The Life and Times of Aaron Burr*, Vol. 1 (New York: Mason Brothers, 1867), p. 267–268.

10. John Ferling, "Thomas Jefferson, Aaron Burr and the Election of 1800," Smithsonian.com (November 1, 2004). https://www.smithsonianmag.com/history/thomas-jefferson-aaron-burr-and-the-election-of-1800-131082359/.

11. Frank Moore, *American Eloquence: A Collection of Speeches and Addresses by the Most Eminent Orators of America*, Vol. 1 (New York: D. Appleton, 1858), p. 432.

12. Robert A. Caro, *Master of the Senate* (New York: Vintage Books, 2003), p. 13.

13. Robert Aitken and Marilyn Aitken, *Law Makers, Law Breakers, and Uncommon Trials* (Chicago: American Bar Association, 2007), p. 41.

14. Nancy Isenberg, *Fallen Founder: The Life of Aaron Burr* (New York: Penguin, 2007), p. 365.

15. Charles Warren, *A History of the American Bar* (Boston: Little, Brown, and Company, 1911), pp. 267–268.

16. Buckner F. Melton, *Aaron Burr: Conspiracy to Treason* (New York: John Wiley & Sons, 2001), p. 219.

CHAPTER 18: NATION'S SERVICE (1808–1825)

1. Oliver Wolcott, Jr., to Frederick Wolcott, Dec. 26, 1808, Litchfield Historical Society, Wolcott Collection.

2. http://founders.archives.gov/documents/Jefferson/03-02-02-0453.

3. Joseph Story, *Life and Letters of Joseph Story* (Boston: Little, Brown, 1851), p. 187.

4. Lynne Cheney, *James Madison: A Life Reconsidered* (New York: Penguin, 2015), p. 373.

5. Maria Campbell and James Freeman Clarke, *Revolutionary Services and Civil Life of General William Hull* (New York: D. Appleton & Co., 1848), p. 395.

6. Spencer Tucker, James R. Arnold, Roberta Wiener, Paul G. Pierpaoli, Jr., and John C. Fredriksen, eds., *The Encyclopedia of the War of 1812: A Political, Social, and Military History*, Vol. 1 (Santa Barbara, CA: ABC-CLIO, 2012), p. 357.

7. http://founders.archives.gov/documents/Madison/03-06-02-0657.

8. Spencer Tucker, *U.S. Leadership in Wartime: Clashes, Controversy, and Compromise*, Vol. 1 (Santa Barbara, CA: ABC-CLIO, 2009), p. 105.

9. David W. Miller, *The Taking of American Indian Lands in the Southeast: A History of Territorial Cessions and Forced Relocations, 1607–1840* (Jefferson, NC: McFarland, 2011), p. 128.

10. Richard K. Crallé, ed., *The Works of John C. Calhoun*, Vol. V, *Reports and Public Letters* (New York: D. Appleton, 1855), pp. 18–19.

11. John Niven, *John C. Calhoun and the Price of Union: A Biography* (Baton Rouge: Louisiana State University Press, 1993), p. 26.

12. Jules Witcover, *The American Vice Presidency: From Irrelevance to Power* (Washington: Smithsonian Books, 2014), p. 69.

CHAPTER 19: NATION'S SERVICE (1826–1836)

1. John C. Calhoun to James Monroe, June 23, 1826, in *The Papers of John C. Calhoun*, Vol. 10, ed. Clyde N. Wilson and W. Edwin Hemphill (Columbia: University of South Carolina Press, 1977), pp. 132–35.

2. See Chapter Eighteen for a description of Porter's military service during the War of 1812.

3. Henry Clay, *The Papers of Henry Clay*, Vol. 7, *Secretary of State, January 1, 1828–March 4, 1829* (Lexington: University Press of Kentucky, 1982), p. 175.

4. Jon Meacham, *American Lion: Andrew Jackson in the White House* (New York: Random House, 2009), p. 126.

5. John C. Calhoun to Virgil Maxcy, September 11, 1830. Galloway-Maxcy-Markoe Papers at Library of Congress.

6. John Sutherland and Stephen Fender, *Love, Sex, Death and Words: Surprising Tales from a Year in Literature* (London: Icon Books Ltd, 2011), p. 70.

7. Washington Irving, *A Tour on the Prairies* (Philadelphia: Carey, Lea & Blanchard, 1835), p. 3.

8. *United States v. David Shive* (1832).

CHAPTER 20: NATION'S SERVICE (1837–1861)

1. https://www.treasury.gov/about/history/pages/lwoodbury.aspx.

2. William Montgomery Meigs, *The Life of John Caldwell Calhoun*, Vol. 2 (New York: Neale Publishing Company, 1917), p. 220.

3. Matthew Karp, *This Vast Southern Empire* (Cambridge, MA: Harvard University Press, 2016), p. 50.

4. Meigs, p. 313.

5. James Knox Polk, *The Diary of James K. Polk During His Presidency, 1845 to 1849*, Vol. 1 (Chicago: A. C. McClurg, 1910), p. 37.
6. Ibid., p. 62.

7. Sidney Blumenthal, *A Self-Made Man: The Political Life of Abraham Lincoln*, Vol. 1, *1809–1849* (New York: Simon and Schuster, 2017), p. 390.

8. John M. Clayton to John J. Crittenden, March 16, 1849, Crittenden MS, Library of Congress.

9. K. Jack Bauer, *Zachary Taylor: Soldier, Planter, Statesman of the Old Southwest* (Baton Rouge: Louisiana State University Press, 1993), p. 286.

10. Horace Mann, *Slavery: Letters and Speeches* (Boston: B. B. Mussey & Company, 1851), p. 204.

11. George Ticknor Curtis, *Life of Daniel Webster*, Vol. 2 (New York: D. Appleton, 1872), p. 478.

12. David T. Dixon, "Augustus R. Wright and the Loyalty of the Heart," *The Georgia Historical Quarterly* 94, no. 3 (Fall 2010), pp. 354–355.

CHAPTER 21: END OF AN ERA

1. Marian C. McKenna, *Tapping Reeve and The Litchfield Law School* (Oceana Publications, 1986), p. 159.

2. Betsey Reeve to John Cotton Smith, April 6, 1820, Reeve Mss., Litchfield Historical Society.

3. Quoted in McKenna, p. 162.

4. William Ennis to Horace Mann, March 4, 1821, Massachusetts Historical Society.

5. Benjamin Tallmadge to John P. Cushman, February 21, 1822, Litchfield Historical Society.

6. Simeon E. Baldwin, "James Gould, 1770–1838," in *Great American Lawyers*, Vol. 2, ed. William Draper Lewis (Philadelphia: John C. Winston Company, 1907), p. 481.

7. For details about the frictions between Reeve and Gould from 1820 to 1823, see McKenna, pp. 165–169.

8. Lyman Beecher, *A Sermon Preached at the Funeral of the Hon. Tapping Reeve* (Litchfield, CT: S. S. Smith, 1827), p. 10.

9. Tapping Reeve to John P. Cushman, January 22, 1819, Litchfield Historical Society.

10. Mckenna, Appendix VI, p. 199.

11. Beecher, *Sermon*, p. 11.

12. McKenna, Appendix VI, p. 202.

13. Quoted in Dwight C. Kilbourn, *The Bench and Bar of Litchfield County, Connecticut, 1709–1909: Biographical Sketches of Members, History and Catalogue of the Litchfield Law School, Historical Notes* (Litchfield, CT: Privately published, 1909), p. 188.

14. Quoted in Thomas Rogers Hunter, "Litchfield on the Savannah: William Tracy Gould and the Deep South's First Law School," *The Journal of Southern Legal History* 19 (2011): 186.

15. John H. Langbein, "Blackstone, Litchfield, and Yale: The Founding of the Yale Law School," in *History of the Yale Law School*, ed. Anthony T. Kronman (New Haven, CT: Yale University Press, 2004), p. 31.

16. Charles Warren, *A History of the American Bar* (Boston: Little, Brown, 1911), p. 363.

17. Faculty of Harvard Law School, *The Centennial History of the Harvard Law School, 1817–1917* (Cambridge, MA: Harvard University Press, 1918), p. 7.

18. Ibid, p. 6.

19. Daniel R. Coquillette and Bruce A. Kimball, *On the Battlefield of Merit: Harvard Law School, the First Century* (Cambridge, MA: Harvard University Press, 2015), p. 53.

20. Joel Parker, *The Law School of Harvard College* (New York: Hurd and Houghton, 1871), p. 8.

Bibliography

Adams, John Quincy. *Documents Relating to New-England Federalism*, edited by Henry Adams. Boston: Little, Brown, 1905.

Aitken, Robert, and Marilyn Aitken. *Law Makers, Law Breakers, and Uncommon Trials*. Chicago: American Bar Association, 2007.

Alschuler, Albert W. "Rediscovering Blackstone." *University of Pennsylvania Law Review* 145 (November 1996).

Ambler, Charles Henry, ed. "Correspondence of Robert M. T. Hunter, 1826–1876." U.S. Government Printing Office, 1918.

Anderson, George Baker. *Landmarks of Rensselaer County*. Syracuse, NY: D. Mason & Company, 1897.

Andrews, William L., and Regina E. Mason, eds. *Life of William Grimes, the Runaway Slave*. New York: Oxford University Press, 2008.

Bagnall, Whitney S. "Composite Curriculum at Litchfield Law School based on lectures of Tapping Reeve, 1790–1798." 2013. https://documents.law. yale.edu/litchfield-law-school-sources/composite-curriculum-litchfield-law-school-based-lectures-tapping-reeve-1790-1798.

———. "Composite Curriculum of Litchfield Law School, 1812–1813." 2013. https://documents.law.yale.edu/litchfield-law-school-sources/com-posite-curriculum-litchfield-law-school-1812-1813.

Baldwin, Simeon. "James Gould, 1770–1838." In *Great American Lawyers*, edited by William Draper Lewis. 8 volumes. Philadelphia: John C. Winston Company, 1907–1909.

Baldwin, Simeon E. "The United States Law Journal of 1822" (1918). Faculty Scholarship Series. Paper 4309. http://digitalcommons.law.yale.edu/fss_papers/4309.

Barrett, Walter. *The Old Merchants of New York City*. New York: Carleton, 1870.

Bauer, K. Jack. "Zachary Taylor: Soldier, Planter, Statesman of the Old Southwest." Baton Rouge: Louisiana State University Press, 1993.

Beck, Karen. "One Step at a Time: The Research Value of Law Student Notebooks." *Law Library Journal* 91, 1 (Winter 1999).

Beecher, Lyman. *A Sermon Preached at the Funeral of the Hon. Tapping Reeve: Late Chief Justice of the State of Connecticut, who Died December Thirteen, Eighteen Hundred and Twenty-Three, in the Eightieth Year of His Age, with Explanatory Notes.* Litchfield, CT: S. S. Smith, 1827.

———. *Autobiography, Correspondence, &c. of Lyman Beecher*, Vol. 1, edited by Charles Beecher. New York: Harper & Brothers, 1864.

———. *The Remedy for Duelling: A Sermon, Delivered Before the Presbytery of Long-Island, at the Opening of Their Session, at Aquebogue, April 16, 1806.* New York: J. Seymour, printer, 1809.

Ben-Atar, Doron S., and Richard D. Brown *Taming Lust.* Philadelphia: University of Pennsylvania Press, 2014.

Billings, Roger. *Abraham Lincoln, Esq.: The Legal Career of America's Greatest President.* Lexington: University Press of Kentucky, 2010.

Blackstone, Sir William. *Commentaries 1.* London: Clarendon Press, 1768.

Blondel-Libardi, Catherine. "Rediscovering the Litchfield Law School Notebooks." *Connecticut History* 46 (Spring 2007).

Blumberg, Phillip. *Repressive Jurisprudence in the Early American Republic: The First Amendment and the Legacy of English Law.* Cambridge: University of Cambridge Press, 2010.

Blumenthal, Sidney. *A Self-Made Man: The Political Life of Abraham Lincoln.* Vol. I, 1809–1849. New York: Simon and Schuster, 2017.

Boardman, David S. *Sketches of the Early Lights of the Litchfield Bar.* Litchfield, CT: James Humphrey, Jr., 1860.

Boonshoft, Mark. "The Great Awakening." In *The American Revolution Reborn*, edited by Patrick Spero and Michael Zuckerman. Philadelphia: University of Pennsylvania Press, 2016.

———. "The Litchfield Network: Education, Social Capital, and the Rise and Fall of a Political Dynasty, 1784–1833." *Journal of the Early Republic* 34, No. 4 (Winter 2014).

Boorstin, Daniel J. *The Mysterious Science of the Law: An Essay on Blackstone's Commentaries.* Chicago: University of Chicago Press, 1941.

Boswell, George C., ed. *Litchfield Book of Days.* Litchfield, CT: 1899.

Briceland, Alan V. "Ephraim Kirby: Pioneer of American Law Reporting, 1789." *The American Journal of Legal History* 16, No. 4 (October 1972).

Burr, Aaron, and Matthew Livingston Davis. *Memoirs of Aaron Burr: With Miscellaneous Selections from His Correspondence*, Vol. 1. New York: Harper and Brothers, 1837.

Burrows, Edwin G., and Mike Wallace. *Gotham: A History of New York City to 1898.* New York: Oxford University Press, 1998.

Butler, Joseph Green. *History of Youngstown and the Mahoning Valley, Ohio,*

Vol. 1. Chicago: American Historical Society, 1921.

Calder, Jacqueline. *Life and Times of Tapping Reeve and his Law School.* Typescript. Litchfield, CT: Litchfield Historical Society, 1978.

Campbell, Maria, and James Freeman Clarke. *Revolutionary Services and Civil Life of General William Hull.* New York: D. Appleton and Co., 1848.

Carley, Rachel. *Litchfield: The Making of a New England Town.* Litchfield, CT: Litchfield Historical Society, 2011.

Caro, Robert A. *Master of the Senate.* New York: Vintage Books, 2003.

Carpenter, Dorr Bradley, ed. *Stephen R. Bradley: Letters of a Revolutionary War Patriot and Vermont Senator.* Jefferson, NC: McFarland, 2008.

Carrington, Paul D. "The Revolutionary Idea of University Legal Education." *William & Mary Law Review* 31 (1990).

———. "The Theme of Early American Law Teaching: The Political Ethics of Francis Lieber." *Journal of Legal Education* 42 (1992).

Catlin, George. *Manners, Customs, and Conditions of the North American Indians.* Courier Corporation, June 1, 1973.

Chaput, Erik J., and Russell DeSimone. *The Road Not Taken: John Brown Francis and the Dorr Rebellion.* Providence College, Digital Commons, 2014. PDF (text searchable). https://digitalcommons.providence.edu/dorr_scholarship/2/.

Chase, Anthony. "Tapping Reeve." In *Yale Biographical Directory of American Law,* edited by Roger K. Newman. New Haven, CT: Yale University Press, 2009.

Chemical Bank and Trust Company. *History of the Chemical Bank: 1823–1913.* Privately printed, 1913.

Cheney, Lynne. *James Madison: A Life Reconsidered.* New York: Penguin, 2015.

Chernow, Ron. *Alexander Hamilton.* New York: Penguin, 2005.

Church, Samuel. "Address." In "Litchfield County Centennial Celebration." Hartford, CT: Edwin Hunt, 1851.

Clay, Henry. *The Papers of Henry Clay,* Vol. 7, *Secretary of State, January 1, 1828–March 4, 1829.* Lexington: University Press of Kentucky, 1982.

Coit, Margaret L. *John C. Calhoun: American Portrait.* Boston: Houghton Mifflin, 1950.

Cole, Donald B. *Martin van Buren and the American Political System.* Princeton, NJ: Princeton University Press, 2014.

Collier, Christopher. "Tapping Reeve, the Connecticut Common Law, and America's First Law School." *Connecticut Supreme Court History,* vol. 1 (2006).

Copland, Laura. "The Rise and Fall of Moses Simons: A Black Lawyer in the

New York City Criminal Court, 1816–1820." *African Americans in New York Life and History*, vol. 37 (2013).

Coquillette, Daniel R., and Bruce A. Kimball. *On the Battlefield of Merit: Harvard Law School, the First Century*. Cambridge, MA: Harvard University Press, 2015.

Crallé, Richard K., ed. *The Works of John C. Calhoun*, Vol. V, *Reports and Public Letters*. New York: D. Appleton, 1855.

Crockett, Walter H. *Vermont: The Green Mountain State*. New York: The Century History Company, 1921.

Cronin, James E., ed. *The Diary of Elihu Hubbard Smith (1771–1798)*. Philadelphia: American Philosophical Society, 1973.

Cumming, Joseph B. "The Cumming-McDuffie Duels," *The Georgia Historical Quarterly* 44, no. 1 (March 1960).

Curtis, George Ticknor. *Life of Daniel Webster*, Vol. 2. New York: D. Appleton, 1872.

Custer, Lawrence B. "The Litchfield Law School: Educating Southern Lawyers in Connecticut." *Georgia Journal of Southern Legal History* 2 (1993).

D. Appleton. *The American Annual Cyclopædia and Register of Important Events of the Year 1870*. New York: D. Appleton, 1871.

Dana, Richard Henry, Jr. "A Tribute to Judge Sprague." Privately printed. Boston: Alfred Mudge & Son, 1864.

Danner, Richard A. "More than Decisions: Reviews of American Law Reports in the Pre-West Era." Duke Law School Public Law & Legal Theory Series No. 2015–27 (June 19, 2015).

Darling, Charles William. *Memorial to my Honored Kindred*. Privately Printed. Utica, NY, 1888.

Devitt, Fred B., Jr. "One Hundred Eightieth Anniversary Feature: William and Mary: America's First Law School." *William & Mary Law Review* 2, issue 2 (1960). https://scholarship.law.wm.edu/wmlr/vol2/iss2/8/.

Dexter, Franklin Bowditch. *Biographical Sketches of the Graduates of Yale College: With Annals of the College History 1701–1815*. 6 volumes. New York: Henry Holt, 1885–1912.

DiLorenzo, Thomas J. "Yankee Confederates: New England Secession Movements Prior to the War Between the States." In *Secession, State and Liberty*, edited by David Gordon. New Brunswick, NJ: Transaction Publishers, 1998.

Dixon, David T. "Augustus R. Wright and the Loyalty of the Heart." *The Georgia Historical Quarterly* 94, no. 3 (Fall 2010).

Dwight, Timothy. *Travels in New-England and New-York*, Vol. 4. London:

William Baynes and Son, 1823.

E. Thompson Company. "The Litchfield Law School." *Law Notes* 4 (1900).

Eiseman, Jason, Whitney Bagnall, Cate Kellett, and Caitlyn Lam. "Litchfield Unbound: Unlocking Legal History with Metadata, Digitization, and Digital Tools." *Law and History Review* 34 (2016): 831.

Faculty of Harvard Law School. *The Centennial History of the Harvard Law School, 1817–1917*. Cambridge, MA: Harvard University Press, 1918.

Farnham, Thomas J. "Tapping Reeve and America's First Law School." *New England Galaxy* 17 (1975): 3–13.

Ferling, John. "Thomas Jefferson, Aaron Burr and the Election of 1800." Smithsonian.com, November 1, 2004. https://www.smithsonianmag.com/history/thomas-jefferson-aaron-burr-and-the-election-of-1800-131082359/.

Fernandez, Angela, "Copying and copyright issues at Litchfield Law School." University of Toronto Legal Studies Research Paper 08-13 (2008). https://papers.ssrn.com/sol3/papers.cfm?abstract_id=1160023.

Fernandez, Angela, and Markus Dubber, eds. *Law Books in Action: Essays on the Anglo-American Legal Treatise*. Portland, OR: Hart Publishing, 2012.

Finkelman, Paul, ed. *The Supreme Court: Controversies, Cases, and Characters from John Jay to John Roberts*, Vol. 1. Santa Barbara, CA: ABC-CLIO, 2014.

Fisher, Samuel H. *The Litchfield Law School: Address by Samuel Fisher*. Litchfield, CT: Litchfield Enquirer Press, 1930.

_____. *Litchfield Law School, 1774–1833: A Biographical Catalogue of Students*. New Haven, CT: Yale University Press, 1946.

_____. *The Litchfield Law School, 1775–1833*. Tercentenary Commission of the State of Connecticut Committee on Historical Publications, XXI. New Haven, CT: Yale University Press, 1933.

_____. "Why Two Connecticut Yankees Went South." *The Florida Historical Quarterly* 18, no. 1 (July 1939).

Friedman, Lawrence M. *A History of American Law*. 3rd ed. New York: Simon and Schuster, 2005.

Gawalt, Gerard W. "Massachusetts Legal Education in Transition, 1766–1840." *The American Journal of Legal History* 17, no. 1 (January 1973).

Goetsch, Charles C. "The Litchfield Law School: A Modern View." Copy of paper at Litchfield Historical Society, Litchfield, CT.

Gould, James. "Law School at Litchfield." *United States Law Journal and Civilian's Magazine*. (1823).

Gunther, Gerald. *Learned Hand: The Man and the Judge*. New York: Oxford University Press, 2010.

Hall, Benjamin Homer. *History of Eastern Vermont: From Its Earliest Settlement to the Close of the Eighteenth Century.* New York: D. Appleton, 1858.

Halow, D. Brooke. "Litchfield's Legacy in Law: A Study of the Litchfield Law School's Influence on Legal Training in America, 1784–1833." *American Studies* 493. Yale University Law School, 1996.

Henson, Margaret Swett. "Trinity Land Company," in Handbook of Texas Online. http://www.tshaonline.org/handbook/online/articles/uft01.

Hicks, Paul DeForest. *Joseph Henry Lumpkin: Georgia's First Chief Justice.* Athens: University of Georgia Press, 2002.

Hill, Burton S. "Litchfield, First American Law School." *Quarterly Review: A Journal of University Perspectives* 56 (1949).

Hill, Walter B. "The Supreme Court of Georgia." *The Green Bag* 4. Boston Book Company, 1892.

Holmes, Oliver Wendell, Jr. *The Common Law.* Boston: Little, Brown, 1909.

Hopkins, Samuel Miles, and Sarah Hopkins Bradford. *Sketch of the Public and Private Life of Samuel Miles Hopkins, of Salem, Connecticut.* Rochester, NY: The Society, 1898.

Horton, Wesley W. *The Connecticut State Constitution.* New York: Oxford University Press, 2012.

Huebner, Timothy S. *The Taney Court: Justices, Rulings, and Legacy.* Santa Barbara, CA: ABC-CLIO, 2003.

Hunt, Freeman, William B. Dana, and Isaac Smith Homans. *Merchants' Magazine and Commercial Review*, Vol. 31 (1854).

Hunter, Thomas Rogers. "Litchfield on the Savannah: William Tracy Gould and the Deep South's First Law School." *The Journal of Southern Legal History* 19 (2011).

H. Z. Williams and Bro. *History of Trumbull and Mahoning Counties,* Vol. 1. Cleveland, OH: H. Z. Williams and Bro., 1882.

Imholt, Robert J. "Timothy Dwight, Federalist Pope of Connecticut." *The New England Quarterly* 73, no. 3 (September 2000).

Irving, Washington. *A Tour on the Prairies.* Philadelphia: Carey, Lea and Blanchard, 1835.

Isenberg, Nancy. *Fallen Founder: The Life of Aaron Burr.* New York: Penguin, 2007.

Jefferson, Thomas. *Autobiography.* New York: G. P. Putnam, 1914.

Jefferson, Thomas, and Henry Augustine Washington, *The Life and Letters of Thomas Jefferson: Being His Autobiography and Select Correspondence.* New York: Edwards, Pratt and Foster, 1858.

Joyce, Craig. "A Curious Chapter in the History of Judicature: *Wheaton v. Peters* and the Rest of the Story (of Copyright in the New Republic)."

Houston Law Review 42 (2005).

Karp, Matthew. "This Vast Southern Empire." Cambridge, MA: Harvard University Press, 2016.

Kilbourn, Dwight C. *The Bench and Bar of Litchfield County, Connecticut, 1709–1909: Biographical Sketches of Members, History and Catalogue of the Litchfield Law School, Historical Notes.* Litchfield, CT: Privately published, 1909.

Kilbourne, Payne Kenyon. *Sketches and Chronicles of the Town of Litchfield, Connecticut.* Hartford, CT: Press of Case, Lockwood and Company, 1859.

Kirby, Ephraim. *Reports of cases adjudged in the Superior Court of Connecticut; with some determinations in the Supreme Court of Errors.* Litchfield, CT: Collier & Adam, 1789.

Klafter, Craig Evan. "The Influence of Vocational Law Schools on the Origins of American Legal Thought, 1779–1829." *The American Journal of Legal History* 37, no. 3 (July 1993).

Kulp, George B. *Families of the Wyoming Valley: Biographical, Genealogical and Historical. Sketches of the bench and bar of Luzerne County, Pennsylvania.* Wilkes-Barre, PA: E. B. Yordy, 1885.

Langbein, John H. "Blackstone, Litchfield, and Yale: The Founding of the Yale Law School." In *History of the Yale Law School,* edited by Anthony T. Kronman. New Haven, CT: Yale University Press, 2004.

————. "Chancellor Kent and the History of Legal Literature." Faculty Scholarship Series. Paper 549, digitalcommons.law.yale.edu/fss papers/ 549 (1993).

Lanman, Charles, *The Life of William Woodbridge.* Washington: Blanchard & Mohun, 1867.

Lehrman Institute. "Daniel S. Dickinson (1806–1884)," in *Mr. Lincoln and New York.* New York: The Lehrman Institute, 2002–2019. http://www.mrlincolnandnewyork.org/new-yorkers/daniel-s-dickinson-1806-1884/.

Levin, Mark. *Men in Black: How the Supreme Court Is Destroying America.* New York: Simon and Schuster, 2006.

Litchfield Historical Society. "Catalogue: Reprint of 1900." Litchfield, CT: Litchfield Enquirer Press, 1900.

————. "Presentation of the Reeve Law School building to the Litchfield Historical Society at Litchfield, Conn., August 22d, 1911." Litchfield, CT: Litchfield Enquirer Press, 1911.

————."The Litchfield Law School, Litchfield, Connecticut: A Brief Historical Sketch." Litchfield, CT: Litchfield Historical Society, 1952.

_____. "The Noblest Study: The Legacy of America's First School of Law. Permanent Exhibition," Tapping Reeve House, Litchfield, CT.

Litchfield Law School. *The Litchfield Law School, 1784–1833.* Litchfield, CT: Press of the Litchfield Enquirer, 1900.

Madsen, Axel. *John Jacob Astor: America's First Multimillionaire.* New York: John Wiley & Sons, 2002.

Mann, Horace. *Slavery: Letters and Speeches.* Boston: B. B. Mussey and Company, 1851.

Mansfield, Edward Deering. *Personal Memories, Social, Political, and Literary: With Sketches of Many Noted People, 1803–1843.* Cincinnati: Robert Clarke & Co., 1879.

Mathews, Lois Kimball. *The Expansion of New England: The Spread of New England Settlement and Institutions to the Mississippi River, 1620–1865.* Boston and New York: Houghton Mifflin, 1909.

McKenna, Marian C. *Tapping Reeve and The Litchfield Law School.* New York: Oceana Publications, 1986.

McLachlan, James. *Princetonians, 1748–1768: A Biographical Dictionary.* Princeton, NJ: Princeton University Press, 2015.

Meacham, Jon. *American Lion: Andrew Jackson in the White House.* New York: Random House, 2009.

Meigs, William Montgomery. *The Life of John Caldwell Calhoun.* New York: Neale Publishing Company, 1917.

Melhorn, Donald F., Jr. "A Moot Court Exercise: Debating Judicial Review Prior to *Marbury v. Madison.*" *Constitutional Commentary* 12 (Winter 1995).

_____. *Lest We be Marshall'd.* Akron, OH: University of Akron Press, 2003.

Melton, Buckner F. *Aaron Burr: Conspiracy to Treason.* New York: John Wiley & Sons, 2001.

Miller, David W. *The Taking of American Indian Lands in the Southeast: A History of Territorial Cessions and Forced Relocations, 1607–1840.* Jefferson, NC: McFarland, 2011.

Miller, Donald L., and Louis P. Masur. "The Rise of Capitalism: The Unseen Hand." Program 7 of *A Biography of America.* WGBH Educational Foundation, 2000. https://www.learner.org/series/biographyofamerica/prog07/transcript/index.html.

Miller, Perry G. *The Life of the Mind in America: From the Revolution to the Civil War.* New York: Harcourt, 1965.

Mohr, James C. *Abortion in America: The Origins and Evolution of National Policy.* New York: Oxford University Press, 1979.

Moore, Frank. *American Eloquence: A Collection of Speeches and Addresses by the*

Most Eminent Orators of America, Vol. 1. New York: D. Appleton, 1858.

Moss, David A. *Democracy*. Cambridge, MA: Harvard University Press, 2017.

Naparsteck, Martin. *The Trial of Susan B. Anthony: An Illegal Vote, a Court-room Conviction and a Step toward Women's Suffrage*. Jefferson, NC: McFarland, 2014.

Niven, John. *John C. Calhoun and the Price of Union: A Biography*. Baton Rouge: Louisiana State University Press, 1993.

Northen, William J., ed. *Men of Mark in Georgia*, Vol. 3. Atlanta: A. B. Caldwell, 1910.

O'Brien, Michael, ed. *All Clever Men, Who Make Their Way: Critical Discourse in the Old South*. Athens: University of Georgia Press, 2008.

Paisley, Donald J. "Lewis Bartholomew Woodruff." In *The Judges of the New York Court of Appeals: A Biographical History*, edited by Hon. Albert M. Rosenblatt. New York: Fordham University Press, 2007. https://www.ny courts.gov/history/legal-history-new-york/luminaries-court-appeals/ woodruff-lewis.html.

Palmer, John McAuley, ed. *The Bench and Bar of Illinois: Historical and Reminiscent*, Vol. 1. Chicago: The Lewis Publishing Co., 1899.

Parker, Joel. *The Law School of Harvard College*. New York: Hurd and Houghton, 1871.

Parks, Joseph Howard. *The House of Blue Light*. Baton Rouge: Louisiana State University Press, 1992.

Parton, James. *The Life and Times of Aaron Burr*. New York: Mason Brothers, 1867.

Pearson, Ellen Holmes. *Remaking Custom: Law and Identity in the Early American Republic*. Charlottesville: University of Virginia Press, 2011.

Peck, William Farley. *History of Rochester and Monroe County, New York: From the Earliest Historic Times to the Beginning of 1907*, Vol. 1. New York: Pioneer Publishing Company, 1908.

Polk, James Knox. *The Diary of James K. Polk During His Presidency, 1845 to 1849*, Vol. 1. Chicago: A. C. McClurg, 1910.

Pruitt, Paul M., Jr., and David I. Durham. *Commonplace Books of Law: A Selection of Law Related Notebooks from the Seventeenth Century to the Mid-Twentieth Century*. Tuscaloosa: University of Alabama Press, 2005.

Purcell, Richard Joseph. *Connecticut in Transition, 1775–1818*. American Historical Association, 1918.

Quincy, Edmund. *Life of Josiah Quincy of Massachusetts*. Boston: Ticknor and Fields, 1868.

Reed, Alfred Zantzinger. *Training for the Public Profession of the Law*. New York City, 1921.

Reeve, Tapping. *The Law of Baron and Femme, of Parent and Child, Guardian and Ward, Master and Servant.* 3rd ed. Albany, NY: W. Gould, 1862.
———. "The Sixth of August or The Litchfield Festival Address." Hartford, CT: Hudson and Goodwin, 1806.

Root, Jesse. *Reports of Cases Adjudged in the Superior Court and Supreme Court of Errors, From July 1789 to June 1798,* Vol. 2. Hartford, CT: Hudson and Goodwin, 1802.

Sandford, Ann. *Reluctant Reformer: Nathan Sanford in the Era of the Early Republic.* Albany: State University of New York Press, 2017.

Scafidel, J. R. "A Georgian in Connecticut: A. B. Longstreet's Legal Education." *The Georgia Historical Quarterly* 61, no. 3 (Fall 1977).

Schell, Francis. *Memoir of the Hon. Augustus Schell.* Privately printed. 1885.

Shaw, Robert B. "The Great Schuyler Stock Fraud." *Railroad History* no. 141 (Autumn 1979).

Sheppard, Steve, ed. "The History of Legal Education in the United States." 2 Vols. Pasadena, CA: Salem Press, Inc., 1999.

Sheppard, Stephen M. "Casebooks, Commentaries, and Curmudgeons: An Introductory History of Law in the Lecture Hall." *Iowa Law Review* 82 (1997): 547.

Siegel, Andrew M. "'To Learn and to Make Respectable Hereafter': The Litchfield Law School in Cultural Context." *New York University Law Review* 73 (1998): 1978–2028.

Story, Joseph. *Life and Letters of Joseph Story.* Boston: Little, Brown, 1851.

Sutherland, John, and Stephen Fender. *Love, Sex, Death and Words: Surprising Tales from a Year in Literature.* London: Icon Books Ltd., 2011.

Swaine, Robert Taylor. *The Cravath Firm and Its Predecessors, 1819–1947,* Vol. 1. Clark, NJ: The Lawbook Exchange, 2007.

Tefft, Benjamin Franklin. *Life of Daniel Webster.* Philadelphia: Porter and Coates, 1854.

Tucker, Phillip Thomas. *America's Forgotten First War for Slavery and Genesis of the Alamo,* Vol. 1. Portland, OR: PublishNation LLC, 2017.

Tucker, Spencer. *U.S. Leadership in Wartime: Clashes, Controversy, and Compromise,* Vol. 1. Santa Barbara, CA: ABC-CLIO, 2009.

Tucker, Spencer, James R. Arnold, Roberta Wiener, Paul G. Pierpaoli, Jr., and John C. Fredriksen, eds. *The Encyclopedia of the War of 1812: A Political, Social, and Military History.* Vol. 1. Santa Barbara, CA: ABC-CLIO, 2012.

Turner, Frederick Jackson. *The Frontier in American History.* New York: Henry Holt, 1921.

Turner, Kathryn. "The Midnight Judges." *University of Pennsylvania Law Review* 109 (1961).

Ullery, Jacob G. *Men of Vermont: An Illustrated Biographical History of Vermonters and Sons of Vermont*. Brattleboro, VT: Transcript Publishing Company, 1894.

Vanderpoel, Emily Noyes. *Chronicles of a Pioneer School from 1792 to 1833: Being the History of Miss Sarah Pierce and her Litchfield School*. Cambridge, MA: Harvard University Press, 1903.

Vaughn, William Preston. *The Anti-Masonic Party in the United States: 1826–1843*. Lexington: University Press of Kentucky, 2015.

Warren, Charles. *A History of the American Bar*. Boston: Little, Brown, 1911.

_____. *History of the Harvard Law School and of Early Legal Conditions in America*, Vol. 1. New York: Lewis Publishing Company, 1908.

_____. *The Supreme Court in United States History*, Vol. 2. Boston: Little, Brown, 1922.

Williams, Donald E., Jr. *Prudence Crandall's Legacy: The Fight for Equality in the 1830s, Dred Scott, and Brown v. Board of Education*. Middletown, CT: Wesleyan University Press, 2014.

Wilson, Clyde N., and W. Edwin Hemphill, eds. *The Papers of John C. Calhoun*, Vol. 10. Columbia: University of South Carolina Press, 1977.

Wilson, James Grant, and John Fiske, eds. *Appleton's Cyclopaedia of American Biography*, Vol 3. New York: D. Appleton and Company, 1887.

Witcover, Jules. *The American Vice Presidency: From Irrelevance to Power*. Washington, DC: Smithsonian Books, 2014.

Woodruff, George Catlin. *History of the Town of Litchfield, Connecticut*. Litchfield, CT: C. Adams, 1845.

Zilversmit, Arthur. "Quok Walker, Mumbet, and the Abolition of Slavery in Massachusetts," *The William and Mary Quarterly* 25, no. 4 (October 1968).

Index